PRACTICAL SOCIAL WORK

Series Editor: Jo Campling

BASW

Editorial Advisory Board:
Terry Bamford, Malcolm Payne, Patrick Phelan,
Peter Riches, Daphne Statham, Jane Tunstill,
Sue Walrond-Skinner and Margaret Yelloly

Social work is at an important stage in its development. All professions must be responsive to changing social and economic conditions if they are to meet the needs of those they serve. This series focuses on sound practice and the specific contribution which social workers can make to the well-being of our society in the 1980s.

The British Association of Social Workers has always been conscious of its role in setting guidelines for practice and in seeking to raise professional standards. The conception of the Practical Social Work series arose from a survey of BASW members to discover where they, the practitioners in social work, felt there was the most need for new literature. The response was overwhelming and enthusiastic, and the result is a carefully planned, coherent series of books. The emphasis is firmly on practice, set in a theoretical framework. The books will inform, stimulate and promote discussion, thus adding to the further development of skills and high professional standards. All the authors are practitioners and teachers of social work representing a wide variety of experience.

PRACTICAL SOCIAL WORK

Series Editor: Jo Campling

BASW

PUBLISHED

Social Work and Mental Handicap
David Anderson

Social Workers at Risk
Robert Brown, Stanley Bute and
Peter Ford

Social Work and Mental Illness
Alan Butler and Colin Pritchard

Residential Work
Roger Clough

Social Work and Child Abuse
David M. Cooper and David Ball

Sociology in Social Work Practice
Peter R. Day

Welfare Rights Work in Social Services
Geoff Fimister

Student Supervision
Kathy Ford and Alan Jones

Computers in Social Work
Bryan Glastonbury

Working with Families
Gill Gorell Barnes

Youth Work
Tony Jeffs and Mark Smith (eds)

Social Work with Old People
Mary Marshall

Applied Psychology for Social Workers
Paula Nicolson and Rowan Bayne

Crisis Intervention in Social Services
Kieran O'Hagan

Social Work with Disabled People
Michael Oliver

Separation, Divorce and Families
Lisa Parkinson

Social Care in the Community
Malcolm Payne

Working in Teams
Malcolm Payne

Effective Groupwork
Michael Preston-Shoot

*Adoption and Fostering:
Why and How*
Carole R. Smith

*Social Work with the Dying and
Bereaved*
Carole R. Smith

Community Work
Alan Twelvetrees

Working with Offenders
Hilary Walker and Bill Beaumont (eds)

FORTHCOMING

Social Work Practice: An Introduction
Veronica Coulshed

Social Work and Local Politics
Paul Daniel and John Wheeler

Anti-Racist Social Work
Lena Dominelli

Family Work with Elderly People
Alison Froggatt

Child Sexual Abuse
Danya Glaser and Stephen Frosh

Women and Social Work
Jalna Hanmer and Daphne Statham

Childhood and Adolescence
Michael Kerfoot and Alan Butler

Court Work
Carole R. Smith, Mary Lane and
Terry Walsh

Social Work and Housing
Gill Stewart with John Stewart

Child Care
Jane Tunstill

Separation, Divorce and Families

Lisa Parkinson

Foreword by Janet Walker

M

MACMILLAN
EDUCATION

First published 1987

Published by
MACMILLAN EDUCATION LTD
Houndmills, Basingstoke, Hampshire RG21 2XS
and London
Companies and representatives
throughout the world

Printed in Hong Kong

ISBN 0–333–40991–4 (hardcover)
ISBN 0–333–40992–2 (paperback)

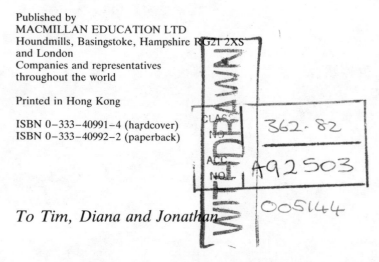
To Tim, Diana and Jonathan

Series Standing Order

If you would like to receive future titles in this series as they are published,
you can make use of our standing order facility. To place a standing order
please contact your bookseller or, in case of difficulty, write to us at the
address below with your name and address and the name of the series.
Please state with which title you wish to begin your standing order. (If you
live outside the United Kingdom we may not have the rights for your area,
in which case we will forward your order to the publisher concerned.)

Customer Services Department, Macmillan Distribution Ltd,
Houndmills, Basingstoke, Hampshire, RG21 2XS, England.

Contents

Foreword by Janet Walker   viii
Acknowledgements   xi
Introduction   xii

1   The Process and Problems of Divorce   **1**
Marriage and divorce trends   1
Changes in parenting and family patterns   3
The status passage of divorce   5
The role of helping agencies   8
Professional monopolies in divorce   10
Conjoint divorce counselling   12
Interrelated dimensions of divorce   14
Divorce and bereavement   22
Joint decisions in divorce   23

2   The Crisis of Separation   **25**
Marriage breakdown, divorce and crisis theory   25
Who is the client?   27
Conjoint interviews in situations of domestic violence?   29
Confidentiality   31
Case study – the Smith family   32
Strategies of crisis intervention   35
Case study – the Brown family   36
Understanding conflict patterns   38
From crisis theory to systems theory   46

v

3 Helping Children Cope with Separation and Divorce   **47**
  Children's reactions to parental separation   48
  Adults and children – a clash of interests?   50
  Interpreting children's reactions   52
  Family dynamics and children's adjustment   55
  Children's roles in family conflict   58
  Reuniting strategies   59
  Case example – running to the other parent   60
  Engaging parents and children simultaneously   61
  The wishes of the child   62
  Communicating with children   63
  Children who refuse access visits   65
  The use of play materials   67
  Groupwork with children   69

4 Who Decides about the Children?   **71**
  Parents' decisions in divorce   71
  Custody decisions   73
  Joint custody   76
  The role of the welfare officer   78
  Case study – the Wilkins family   81
  Mediating between private and public decision-making   83
  Assessment   83
  Intractable conflict   86
  Different approaches to the inquiry task   88
  Welfare inquiries, conciliation and mediation   89

5 Conflict Management and Conciliation   **93**
  Conciliation and mediation   93
  Organisational settings for conciliation   95
  National Family Conciliation Council   98
  The boundaries of conciliation   98
  Imbalances in conciliation   100
  Co-working in conciliation   101
  Different models of co-working   103
  Conciliation – basic tasks   108
  Convening hostile couples   108

New partners and cohabitees   110
Gathering relevant facts   112
Containing and pre-empting conflict   114
The need to disagree   116
Re-framing   117

6 Family Problems after Divorce   **119**
The incomplete emotional divorce   121
Matrimonial supervision orders – a neglected area
of social work practice   122
Statutory powers under matrimonial supervision orders   124
The purpose of matrimonial supervision orders   125
Whom do supervising officers see as their client?   126
Brief work under a matrimonial supervision order   127
Case study 1 – the Thomas family   127
Psychological parenting after divorce   130
Some common problems in stepfamilies   132
Case study 2 – the Walker family   134
Support for stepfamilies   135

7 Family Courts and Social Work Services   **136**
The Family Courts Campaign   136
Social work services in the family court   139
Children's panels and reporters in Scotland   143
Family conferences and network meetings   144
A new family court welfare service   146
Training for court welfare work and conciliation   147
Liaison and joint work with other agencies   154
Educating children in conflict management   156

Appendix A   Some Books about Divorce for Children   157
Appendix B   Some Useful Addresses   158
References   159
Index   170

Foreword

In the late 1980s there are probably few families in Britain whose lives are not touched directly or indirectly by separation and divorce. What was until recently a private issue is now a matter of public concern. For many years the *consequences* of divorce have brought families to the attention of social workers, who have been well aware of the difficulties experienced by many single-parent households. It is, however, only in recent years that attention has been focused on the *process* of separation and divorce and the gap in social work provision for families experiencing major upheaval. Research has clearly shown that the long-term impact of the experience is dependent on the way in which the process is handled, and that the greater the bitterness and conflict surrounding the process the poorer the prognosis for successful adjustment for all family members. It seems to follow, therefore, that social welfare intervention should properly be available for families at the early stage of separation, encouraging social work practitioners to be proactive rather than merely reactive.

In the last ten years new conciliation/mediation services have attempted to fill this gap, adapting social work theories and skills. In this book the possibilities for effective social work with separating families are explored and discussed by a practitioner who has already made a major contribution to the development of conciliation services in Britain. Lisa Parkinson is best known for her pioneering work as the first co-ordinator of the Bristol Courts Family Conciliation Service, in which she established a distinct way of working with separating couples who experience difficulty in agreeing about future arrangements for children. By controlling conflict, parents are enabled to continue to parent whilst letting go of the marriage.

Since these early beginnings Lisa Parkinson has been a tireless campaigner for new innovations in the divorce process, and as Training Officer for the National Family Conciliation Council has run workshops, training sessions and given advice to a range of professional groups throughout Britain. In addition she has presented papers at multidisciplinary conferences in Europe, North America and Britain. She has now written a straightforward and practical guide to the needs of separating families and to the help that social workers can give them. The complex process of separation and adjustment to new family structures is carefully described with an imaginative use of case studies which clearly focus on practice skills and issues. The Smiths and the Browns will be well known to most practitioners, and by understanding the communication patterns, the feelings and the struggles of these couples we can consider the different skills which social workers can use to move people on from the 'stuck' positions which can be so damaging for all family members.

Concern to promote 'the best interests' of children is a well-established principle both in law and in social work practice. Social workers will welcome the author's extensive discussion about the needs of children. Research has shown, painfully clearly at times, how children are seldom listened to or understood by adults and are often left to cope alone with tremendous hurt, guilt and bewilderment. Social workers are all too familiar with situations in which children become a football to be kicked around by warring parents, or are divided up and shared out along with the television and the washing-machine. Social workers have a key role in preventing such situations, and here Lisa Parkinson describes a range of ways of working with children and families which go beyond statutory supervisory duties.

Although a staunch supporter of the conciliation movement, the author is well able to stand back from her own practice to consider the very real dilemmas faced by social workers. Who decides about children? Is it a parental task or a social work role? Can confidentiality and privilege be maintained when social workers are required to protect children and to safeguard their interests? These issues and concerns are not unique to Britain. As the impact of divorce and the consequent changes in family structures become increasingly common throughout the western world knowledge and skills are being shared and developed across international boundaries.

Lisa Parkinson suggests that the paucity of social work literature about separation and divorce may be because professionals have ambivalent feelings about working with these families. Undoubtedly it can be stressful and demanding, requiring practitioners to recognise their own reactions and feelings. While matrimonial work has often not received the attention it deserves, the development of a systemic orientation has uncovered exciting possibilities for highly innovative interventions with divorcing families encouraging joint work across professional groups which the author recognises as an important way forward. As she points out, clarity about principles and objectives helps professionals to select appropriate methods of working and to develop skills in using them. This book will help social welfare practitioners in Britain and elsewhere to do just that. The author has found the right balance between knowledge based on sound research evidence and the practical application of social work skills to enable social workers to advance their own understanding and expertise with separating and divorcing families.

JANET WALKER
Co-Director, Conciliation Project Unit
Chairperson, Association for Family Therapy

Acknowledgements

I should like to thank the friends and colleagues who helped me greatly by reading and commenting on draft chapters of this book, especially Yvonne Craig, Brian Fellowes, Thelma Fisher, Adrian James, Jan Walker and Tony Wells. I should also like to express particularly warm thanks to Sue Walrond-Skinner for her sound judgement and personal encouragement as I struggled to compress a lot of material into one short book. I was extremely fortunate to have Sue as consultant and her editorial expertise has been invaluable. Jonathan Whybrow of the Law Commission gave me a great deal of help with statistics and I am indebted to Molly Knowles of the Frontenac Family Referral Service, Kingston, Ontario, Canada for permission to reproduce the table on page 142.

I should like to thank Fran Dixon and Patrick Joyce of Avon Social Services and Pam McPhee, then with Avon Probation Service, for working with me on our project on the use of matrimonial supervision orders in Avon. The names used in the case studies are fictitious and certain details have been changed so that the actual families on which they are based cannot be recognised in any way.

Finally, but also first and foremost, I should like to thank my husband Tim for combining wizardry with word processors with patience, good humour and willingness to share domestic chores. His support made it possible for me to write this book while continuing to be involved in conciliation developments.

LISA PARKINSON

Introduction

Social workers who work for brief or extended periods with separating and divorced parents and their children cannot remain impervious to the grief, anger and fear which commonly accompany family break-up. The impact of these strong emotions can arouse mixed feelings in those who seek to help – of wanting to alleviate the family's pain whilst feeling disturbed and maybe impotent in the face of so much human distress. We may try to distance ourselves emotionally as we search for rational solutions to conflicts that are generally far from rational. Adults faced with the breakdown of their marriage or equally close relationship often feel as though they have been knocked to the ground and dragged along by a tidal wave of confused and often primitive emotions – grief, rage, jealousy, despair and sometimes even murderous hatred. Attempts to rescue the victims of these destructive forces can be dangerous for the would-be rescuer as well. The attempt may arouse deep anxieties of getting out of our own emotional depth, swamped by currents of feeling we cannot direct or control. The safest course, perhaps, is to avoid getting our feet wet at all. Mattinson and Sinclair (1979) found that many local authority social workers were reluctant to focus directly on their clients' marital problems, even where there were strong practical reasons for doing so. The conflicts of divorce may be even more distressing for workers who are often pulled first one way and then another in their attempts to help children as well as their parents. We need confidence and courage, resilience and strong support from colleagues if we venture into this challenging but not inevitably depressing field of work.

Professionals' ambivalent feelings about working with families during separation and divorce may partially explain the sparsity of social work literature on this subject. Despite the heavily publicised increase in divorce in the last twenty years, books focusing on family reorganisation and adjustment after divorce have been slow in appearing. Early studies were mainly retrospective, describing individuals' difficulties in coming to terms with separation or divorce, rather than how to help families cope with present stresses in planning for the future. Hart (1976) explored what she called 'the sheer anarchy of marital breakdown' (p. 125), the lack of institutional agencies and rituals to help divorcing couples traverse the hazardous 'status passage' from marriage to divorce. Wallerstein and Kelly (1980) made us painfully aware of the impact of divorce on children as well as on their parents, emphasising the high risks it can entail for children's psychological, emotional and intellectual development. By and large, professional literature, like the media, has tended to paint a black picture of divorce, or at least a very grey one. There is then a danger that the social work response to separation and divorce is coloured by negative expectations, with the result that we may heighten parents' anxieties and guilt instead of increasing their ability to cope.

If, on the other hand, we can help parents deal with immediate priorities while maintaining some hope for the future, we may be able to buttress them during a period of crisis that often affects every area of their lives. The starting-point of this book is therefore an optimistic belief that short-term, structured work can help divorcing families find ways of coping and surviving, although inevitably there will be personal suffering and practical problems that we may scarcely touch. In taking this positive approach, I am aware of the risks of glossing over difficulties and making apparent remedies sound too easy. Early intervention is important but many families are referred to social workers only at a late stage, after a great deal of hurt and loss have been suffered. Parents themselves are only likely to look for help at an early stage if they are aware that help exists and if they perceive the help as useful and non-stigmatising. The physical location and public image of agencies offering help to divorcing families need to be considered carefully, if they are to be acceptable to the great majority who would rightly object to being seen as 'problem families'. Instead of assuming that divorce involves some kind of failure or pathology, we need to recognise that conflict can have positive as well as negative functions and that separation need not be damaging.

It has often been pointed out that divorce is an important public issue as well as an intensely private experience. Public beliefs about marriage and divorce and the controls exercised by the law and the courts impinge on people's private lives, raising many questions about the changing roles of men and women, the role of the state and the effects of high unemployment. It is clearly not possible in a short book about social work practice in separation and divorce to discuss major social and economic issues in any depth: I have included some references to books and articles which deal with them more fully. Another subject which needs much more discussion than I can give it here is the pluralist nature of modern Britain, its diversity of cultural and ethnic traditions and the lack of generally accepted norms to guide individual behaviour and attitudes. Some commentators refer to 'marriage' and 'the family' in the singular, as though there were just one type of marriage or family which everyone knows about. However, even a casual observer can see that marriages and families in Britain today encompass many different structures, attitudes and patterns. Members of ethnic minority groups move between two or more cultural worlds and even if they have no language problems, they may be baffled and intimidated by British institutions and bureaucracy. In a multicultural society, there are few norms to define the roles and obligations of wives and husbands, mothers, fathers and step-parents in marriage and in divorce. This makes it much harder for professionals to be clear about what they are trying to achieve and for whom, when parents disagree about the upbringing of their children. We need to stand back, although there is little time to do so, to question our own values and the values of our agencies, as we may otherwise impose values on families which may be quite inappropriate for them.

There is therefore an additional aim in this book to provoke some harder thinking about values and assumptions which underpin social work practice with divorced and remarried families. The image of the traditional nuclear family – a married couple with dependent children – although atypical of the majority of British families today, or possibly ever (Anderson, 1983), still influences our view of what families ought to be like, even if the parents are separated or divorced. Many professionals believe that 'parents are forever' and that divorce does not end parenthood but it is often difficult to be clear who belongs within a so-called reconstituted family and who does not. Should cohabitees and step-parents be included in discussions about the children, and whose children are they? Should other influential members of the family be invited too, or kept in the background? In Asian families, marital conflict is by no means the concern of the two spouses alone. Divorce risks dishonour to the whole family, especially to the wife, who would normally expect her father and brothers to come to her defence if she feels mistreated by her husband and his family (Ballard, 1983). One of the main practical questions addressed in this book is the one that social workers constantly face of deciding who their 'client' is – individuals who seek help, couples, children, nuclear families, wider systems?

Social work with separated or divorcing families confronts us with their personal chaos and the normlessness of the society in which we live. To keep some sense of order in the midst of all this disorder, we need to set our work in some kind of conceptual context or framework, so that we can offer a consistent and reliable response to individual families and understand their problems from more than one point of view. The first chapter of the book outlines the various dimensions of the divorce process and the way professionals tend to work mainly within one dimension, in a fragmented or unco-ordinated way. The second chapter discusses crisis intervention in the early stages of separation, and the third concentrates on children's needs and ways of helping them cope with separation or divorce. Lip-service is often paid to 'the best interests of the child': in practice, children's feelings are often ignored or misunderstood both by their parents and by professionals (Mitchell, 1985). New approaches, many of them interdisciplinary, are being developed to make divorce less traumatic and conflictual for families and this brings us to the subject of conciliation. Conciliation services have mushroomed at a great rate in the last ten years and this speed has added to the confusion about conciliation practice. It is gradually becoming clearer that conciliation is not just a new name for the work many of us have been doing for years in a variety of settings. As a new discipline which crosses traditional boundaries, conciliation gives rise to territorial rivalries between professionals as well as enthusiasm for shared objectives. The final chapter of the book looks towards the creation of a unified family court which could bring conciliation, mediation, welfare inquiries and the work of guardians *ad litem* under the umbrella of a specialist service serving the community as well as the court.

In some situations of family break-up, relationships break down between children and both their parents, not only between the children and one parent and between the parents themselves. Although childcare issues and child abuse are not within the scope of this book, being the subject of other books in this series, I have sought to question some apparent contradictions in social work thinking and practice in different kinds of family break-up. For example, access to children in divorce is usually given high priority by social workers, whereas parental access to children in care seems to be given low priority even where there are strong reasons for maintaining parental contact. This apparent contradiction is raised in Chapter 6 as an issue needing further exploration and discussion.

Social workers need good support themselves if they are to go on caring for others in situations that take an enormous toll of their physical energy, patience and capacity to understand behaviour that may seem selfish, irrational or simply vindictive. Co-working can reduce the strains that individual workers often experience in working with deeply divided families. Different models of co-working are considered as a means of developing strategic interventions as well as providing more support for the workers. As an American therapist (Hancock, 1980, p. 27) has tellingly observed:

> The dimensions of meaning and belonging are at the core of the experience of separation and divorce; they form the arc

of relatedness to others, the bonds we all need to live. Divorce transforms and shifts these bonds. Each person feels its meaning differently; belonging is an issue for each. Links within the family, and connections to the broader social realm, can only be recreated over a long period of time. The family needs temporary buttressing while new foundations are laid, new beams put into place.

In helping separating and divorcing families manage their conflicts while they reorganise their lives and plan for the future, social workers can offer them some temporary buttressing which they may otherwise look for in vain. The pressures of large-scale divorce are stimulating new practical initiatives in many parts of the country and new connections are being made across professional disciplines. I hope this book will encourage readers to make these connections both in conceptual and practical terms, or at least reinforce those they have already made.

1

The Process and Problems of Divorce

Marriage and divorce trends

The dramatic increase in divorce that has taken place in the last twenty years has many direct and indirect consequences for social workers. Whatever setting they work in, they are bound to be involved with many parents and children who have experienced separation or divorce at some stage of their lives. The divorce rate in England and Wales increased sixfold between 1960 and 1980 and the number of couples who divorced in the 1970s was three times the number who divorced in the previous decade (Kiernan, 1983, p. 27). This sharp increase levelled out in the late seventies but the trend is still upwards. In 1985, there were over 160 000 divorces in England and Wales involving almost as many children under 16 – a total of nearly half a million people in that year alone (OPCS, 1986b). Many couples live together without marrying but the marked increase in cohabitation has not affected the divorce rate perceptibly, since cohabitation is often a prelude to marriage rather than an alternative life-style (Kiernan, 1983, p. 23). Marriage as an institution remains very popular and the experience of divorce does not necessarily deter people from marrying again. As many as 80 per cent of those divorcing under the age of thirty remarry within five years and on current trends it is estimated that around one in five men will have married at least twice by the year 2000 (Leete and Anthony, 1979). Remarriages are however rather less stable than first marriages: statistically, they are more likely to end in divorce than first marriages occurring at similar ages

1

(OPCS, 1984a). In 1985, 22 per cent of divorces in England and Wales involved a re-divorce for one or both partners, compared with 9 per cent in 1971 (OPCS, 1986b).

Divorce statistics hit the headlines at regular intervals, often accompanied by 'gloom and doom' pronouncements about the disintegration of families and the loss of commitment to marriage as a lifelong contract. Those who fear that moral standards are collapsing in a society that has lost its traditional values may lament, like Yeats, that

> Things fall apart; the centre cannot hold;
> Mere anarchy is loosed upon the world.

W. B. Yeats, *The Second Coming*

Social research over the last twenty years suggests however that unfavourable comparisons between the present and the recent past may be misleading. The supposed golden age of the nuclear family – married couples living together with their children in stable communities – may be closer to myth than historical reality (Anderson, 1983). High mortality rates up to the middle of this century brought many marriages to an early end, while the number which ended informally in separation cannot be compared with today's figures, since they are not recorded. Stone (1977) suggested that remarriage rates in the seventeenth century following the death of one partner may have been nearly as high as they are today, following divorce. The factors which contribute to divorce are numerous and complex and this book does not set out to explore them in any depth or detail. It is worth noting, however, that couples marrying today expect marriage to bring them companionship and personal happiness, whereas couples in previous generations were generally content if their partner performed adequately as breadwinner or home-maker (Gorer, 1971). High expectations of marital happiness may turn more quickly to recriminations and disillusionment, if reality fails to match the expectations.

These problems are by no means confined to Britain, since most developed countries have experienced similar increases in divorce in the last twenty years. The two countries with the highest divorce rates in the world – the United States and the

Soviet Union – could scarcely differ more in their political, economic and social systems. In California, high divorce rates are often attributed to the pressures of a fast-moving, relatively affluent society and to the growth of the women's movement, while in the Soviet Union divorce is associated with housing shortages, alcoholism among men and the frustrations caused by spending long periods each day standing in queues (Moskoff, 1983). The stress factors vary but when, as often happens, one partner seeks a divorce against the other's wishes, the conflict between them can have severe repercussions on their children, other family members and professionals who become involved in their difficulties. The conflicts of family break-up are not only individual and personal: they often reflect and are intensified by deep divisions in society. This tangle of public and private issues makes it even harder for divorcing couples to deal with their antagonistic feelings towards each other whilst remaining joint parents of their children.

Changes in parenting and family patterns

Family patterns are changing rapidly as a result of large-scale divorce. Attitudes to parenting both within marriage and after divorce may however be slow to catch up with changes in family structure, since our ideas about parental roles are conditioned to a large extent by unquestioned beliefs and value systems. We may even cling to traditional ideas about parenting because they provide a bulwark of security in a shifting, uncertain world. Sociologists and others often refer to the changing role of women in society today, but some commentators (Burgoyne, 1985) have pointed out that many aspects of women's lives have actually changed very little. Throughout this century, it has been generally assumed in Britain that women should be the primary caretakers of their children and that women and children should be economically dependent on men. These assumptions are deeply rooted in the traditions of a patriarchal society and their influence can be traced in the concepts and practice of many different professional disciplines. For example, they are inherent in psychoanalytic theory with its strong focus on the mother-child relationship. In its turn, psychoanalytic theory has influenced theories of child development and the practice of social work and counselling. The imagery of Christianity emphasises the closeness of mother and child. An intimate relationship between father and child may be seen as less important for the child and possibly dispensable, provided the mother-child relationship is intact. This unequal valuation of motherhood and fatherhood has profound implications for the restructuring of families after divorce. It may partially explain why as many as one third of children of divorce lose touch with one parent – usually, their father – soon after their parents separate (Mitchell, 1985).

It is often assumed that fathers are less committed than mothers to parenting their children and that they need to demonstrate their parenting skills, whereas maternal competence is assumed to exist unless it is demonstrably lacking. A father's wish to play an active part in looking after his children may be seen as a threat to the mother's central role, rather than as a source of strength and support for her as well as for the children. When parents separate, the split between them may be deepened by the belief that it is usually the 'good', caring parent who remains with the children and the 'bad' or inadequate parent who leaves home. Although we may be reluctant to acknowledge these judgmental attitudes, the way we actually work with separated parents suggests that they are pervasive and that in many ways we find them convenient. It is much less stressful to accept one partner's version of 'the truth' than to disentangle conflicting versions, and much more comfortable to form a supportive alliance with one parent than to undertake conjoint work with warring parents who involve you in their pain and anger and try to pull you in different directions.

An American therapist (Ahrons, 1980) has suggested that the prevailing belief that divorce and family dissolution are synonymous is probably the strongest deterrent to the development of a theoretical framework for working with separated and divorced families. Without such a theoretical framework, professional intervention can maintain outdated and divisive practices without being challenged to develop a new approach. The very terms we use to describe separated families are value-laden. We talk about 'children from broken homes', although the relationships in some nominally intact families may be more fractured than in some divorced ones. The term 'one-parent family' implies that the family contains only one parent, yet in most one-parent families the other parent is still alive. Why should a divorced or unmarried father not count as a parent if he cares deeply about his children and feels responsible for them? Although the term 'single parent' may accurately describe many situations in which the father (or much less often, the mother) has withdrawn or disappeared completely, this is by no means the case with all divorced families. We should make a distinction between one-parent households and one-parent families, since there is some evidence (see Chapter 4) that the way we label families affects parents' attitudes and behaviour. Divorced fathers who are made to feel redundant may be inclined to give up altogether, while single parents may feel under pressure to prove they are super-parents. Step-parents, too, suffer from the double messages we give them. A step-parent is an instant parent who is often expected to replace an absent natural parent and provide financial support for a child of the family, yet in other ways a step-parent is a non-parent without legal rights (Masson, 1984). Other terms are missing altogether to describe the increasingly complex strands of family relationships, such as an affectionate name with which stepchildren can address a stepgrandparent.

The status passage of divorce

Members of nuclear families do not usually need to define their relationship with each other because relationships between fathers, mothers, sons and daughters are familiar in both senses of the word, whatever experiences and feelings they give rise to. However, defining relationships after separation or divorce is an important and often neglected task. Concepts of family structure and functioning derived from family therapy (Walrond-Skinner, 1976) are particularly helpful in understanding the emotional tasks and transitional processes of divorce. Minuchin (1974) and others conceived the family as an interacting system in which certain patterns of behaviour have a function for the family as a whole as well as for its individual members. He noted that the functioning of this family system was greatly affected by the functioning of two sub-systems: the marital sub-system and the parental sub-system. In theory, these sub-systems are separate but in practice they are closely intertwined and conflict easily spreads from one to the other. When a couple cannot manage to co-operate either as marital partners or as parents, parent–child relationships are likely to be severely affected, as well as those between the children and other family members. Families may then need professional help in clarifying and restructuring their relationships whilst also attending to urgent practical problems.

As Hart (1976) showed in her sensitive study of the divorce experience, the process of marital dissolution is not marked by discrete transitional statuses indicating the beginning, middle and end of the process. Divorcing couples may not even be sure when they are legally divorced, as the divorce decree is granted in two stages, the decree nisi and the decree absolute. At the time of writing, a decree absolute of divorce is not granted automatically after a period of time but has to be applied for separately. Divorce statistics show that in about 3000 divorces per year (England and Wales) neither partner applies for the decree absolute. Although some of these couples may have reconciled, those who remain half-married and half-divorced may experience prolonged and acute distress (see Chapter 6). Hart found that the status passage from marriage to divorce is characterised by 'attenuated uncertainty' and by a lack of guide-lines and role support for couples attempting to traverse this emotional no-man's land. Marriage and parenthood are major sources of identity and social status. Individuals who lose their identity as spouse and parent without finding an alternative source of identity and social position may become seriously depressed and even lose the will to live.

Holmes and Rahe (1967) developed a scale of stressful life events which showed that people experiencing high levels of

stress are more likely to become ill. Their scale was con-
structed by asking 400 subjects to rate different life events
according to the degree of life change they thought they
involved. Divorce scored second only to death of a spouse as a
life-changing event, higher than imprisonment, dismissal
from work, retirement, pregnancy or the death of a close
friend. Admission rates to psychiatric hospitals and suicide
rates are much higher for the divorced and separated than for
the married or never married (Morgan, 1979) and divorced
women report a greatly increased incidence of depressive
illness and stress-related physical symptoms, especially
around the time of their separation (Chester, 1971). An
abandoned wife may feel devastated and extremely bitter
because her husband has apparently walked away from their
marriage and family, leaving her to struggle on alone. A
number of studies (Ambrose, Harper and Pemberton, 1983;
Jordan, 1985; Kressel, 1985) show however that many
divorced men also suffer very great distress. Their distress
may be longer-lasting because men commonly find it hard to
acknowledge and articulate their feelings and they are less
likely than women to seek help with emotional difficulties.

These studies provide strong evidence that divorce is
associated with higher than average rates of mental and
physical disorder. We must be careful however not to assume
that divorce itself causes these ill-effects. Critical mediating
factors include the reasons for the divorce, the way decisions
are taken and the way the divorce process is managed and
experienced. People can cope with high levels of stress if they
are adequately supported and divorce may lead to greatly
improved physical health and far greater happiness. If,
however, individuals feel devalued and crushed by forces
which grind along with no concern for their survival, the
effects on their emotional and physical health are bound to be
very severe. Unresolved grief and anger from a broken
marriage can cast very long shadows and there is usually acute
financial as well as emotional distress. More than half the one
million single-parent households in this country are on
supplementary benefit, compared with only 10 per cent of
two-parent households (Family Policy Studies Centre, 1987).

The role of helping agencies

Despite the severity and prevalence of these problems, social work with separating and divorcing families has attracted little attention until recently. Perhaps part of the reason is that marital and family problems often touch on sensitive areas of our own experience, as adults or as children. Professionals may also disagree among themselves about the kind of help that is needed, with the result that different agencies or institutions sometimes mirror the dynamics of the conflicted family. Divorcing couples themselves often take up entrenched positions, each spouse seeking to enlist other people who will take up the cudgels on their behalf and help them defeat their former partner. While adults fight out their personal battles, children may be left to make their own way backwards and forwards across the emotional minefield which divides warring couples and their supporters.

Like many other private and public issues in this country, divorce has traditionally been handled in a divisive way which exacerbates the conflicts of divorcing couples instead of alleviating them. Generally speaking, public opinion in Britain has become more tolerant of divorce as the remedy for a failed marriage and the social stigma associated with divorce has faded. However, there is still a tendency to blame one partner for the break-up and to see the other as the victim, on the basis of limited and usually one-sided information. Professionals are not immune to these powerful currents of sympathy or alienation and social workers may get caught in their emotional undertow without necessarily recognising their source. Consequently, when we undertake work with divorcing or divorced individuals and their families, our response may convey unspoken messages at a very early stage in our contact with them. There may be an implicit message in the title of our agency – a title that may be so familiar to us that we take it for granted, forgetting how judgmental it may sound to those who contact the agency for the first time.

Many marriage guidance counsellors offer counselling for divorce as well as for marriage but the title 'Marriage

Guidance' is then inappropriate and may increase feelings of guilt and failure among those whose marriage has broken down. Follow-up studies of marriage guidance clients (Mitchell, 1981; Brannen and Collard, 1982; Hunt, 1985) show that many are desperate to achieve a reconciliation with a partner who has already left and/or started divorce proceedings. In Brannen and Collard's study, some couples had already separated by the time the first counselling session took place and counselling generally ceased after two sessions, without the second partner attending at all. If counselling agencies are perceived as primarily concerned to repair broken marriages, those intent on divorce will probably avoid them even though they may be suffering extreme anxiety and distress. Only 3 per cent of marriage guidance referrals in 1982 were made by solicitors (Tyndall, 1985) suggesting that once legal proceedings are contemplated or under way, marriage guidance is either not considered or not accepted. Considering the large numbers who divorce, there would seem to be great need for doors clearly marked 'divorce counselling', offering access to practical information as well as help with the emotional problems of divorce.

Divorce counsellors must be careful however not to treat divorcing people as clients in need of treatment, therapy or welfare help. This would convey negative assumptions from the start, making those who consult them feel inferior and inadequate when faced with professionals who have expertise, authority and possibly statutory powers as well. Social workers and probation officers are often encouraged by families and the courts to accept that couples who cannot live together as man and wife are incapable of taking joint decisions about their children. If the parents themselves cannot agree, each of them may want some authority to take control and tell the other parent what to do. Fighting over the children allows adults to battle over other matters that may have very little to do with the children themselves. At another level, the battle may reflect differences of view about the roles of men and women in society and the extent to which separated parents should retain responsibilities towards each other and their children.

Professional monopolies in divorce

The emotional problems of separation and divorce are often compounded by professional monopolies and vested interests which make the process more disjointed and bewildering than it need be. Doctors, lawyers and social workers cannot be equally competent in each other's discipline but research findings suggest that professionals regard other disciplines with considerable suspicion and sometimes overt hostility. Borkowski, Murch and Walker (1983) found in their study of marital violence that profound problems could result from differences of professional ethos. 'All communication involves the problems of crossing boundaries. Our medical, legal, and social care systems may be conceived of as three distinct worlds, each with a different specialist language and set of professional values' (p. 178).

The multi-disciplinary help which people need during separation and divorce is not readily available and they may even be actively discouraged from looking for it. Professionals who fail to suggest other possible sources of help may be ill-informed, overworked and/or concerned to control whatever action is taken. They may be anxious to guard their own professional territory and reluctant to share their clients with others. Chester's research (1971) showed that approximately three-quarters of the divorced women in his sample had consulted their family doctor concerning a serious deterioration in their health prior to and following separation: most of them received some form of drug treatment. There was little evidence of doctors seeking to refer both partners or former partners to other helping agencies, although 'general practitioners may be strategically located to mediate in situations of marriage breakdown, possibly by referral to social workers' (p. 235).

Statutory welfare agencies may be shunned because of their stigmatising associations with poverty or crime and their powers to receive children into care. A representative study of divorce petitioners conducted by researchers at Bristol University from 1972 to 1975 (Borkowski, Murch and Walker, 1983) found that 42 per cent of the wife petitioners and 20 per cent of the husband petitioners had consulted their family doctor but only a very small minority had contacted other helping agencies. Only 7 per cent had seen a local authority social worker or probation officer, 5 per cent a voluntary social worker or school teacher, 2 per cent a minister of religion and 1 per cent a marriage guidance counsellor. Similar findings were reported in a study based on a self-selected sample of divorced men (Ambrose, Harper and Pemberton, 1983), who were asked what sources of help and support they had turned to and how much help they felt they had received. Parents, siblings, friends and colleagues at work were all very significant sources of help, whereas doctors, lawyers, ministers of religion and other formal services were generally found less helpful and supportive. 'The social services generally . . . were found to be of least assistance, with definitely unhelpful responses heavily outweighing helpful ones' (p. 68).

Almost all divorce petitioners seek legal advice and the majority find their solicitors helpful (Davis, Macleod and Murch, 1982), although much depends on what kind of help they are looking for. 'Helpful' solicitors may take on one or more of several possible roles, depending on their assessment of the situation and the concerns or instructions of their clients. A solicitor who fires off sharply worded letters to the other party's solicitor may be welcomed by an angry spouse who is determined to defeat a former partner, whereas other divorcing individuals may want a more neutral or conciliatory approach. The way solicitors and the courts handle disputes arising from separation and divorce has changed considerably in recent years and the legal process of divorce has become less adversarial. However, lawyers focus mainly on legal and financial matters and it is not part of the solicitor's responsibility to help couples divorce each other emotionally and psychologically as well as legally. A legal system which encourages divorcing couples to communicate by proxy via their solicitors does not help them work through the emotional and psychological tasks of ending their marriage. In fact, by enabling them to avoid these tasks it may leave them still married to each other at an emotional level, despite having a decree absolute of divorce. Two Swedish therapists, Bente and Gunnar Oberg (1982) have suggested that confrontation need not be destructive and that the avoidance of confrontation may prolong bitterness and distress for one or both partners. Face-to-face discussions, though often distressing and painful, may clear up misunderstandings and reduce harmful fantasies, provided enough support is available to keep the discussions under control. Otherwise, anger and resentment may continue to fester and more pressure may be put on children, other relatives and professionals to carry messages, demands or threats backwards and forwards between the two 'principals'. Professionals who intervene too forcefully or protectively may even collude with parents who seek to abdicate their responsibility for decisions to formal institutions, such as the court.

Conjoint divorce counselling

Most studies of the divorce experience have focused on individual reactions and adjustment to the past (Chester, 1971; Hart, 1976; Ambrose, Harper and Pemberton, 1983) without considering the interactions that are taking place in the present. Bernard's (1973) observation that each marriage contains two subjective experiences of the marriage – the husband's and the wife's – is even more true in relation to divorce, where one partner's account of the breakdown and subsequent events often directly contradicts the other's. The conflicting perceptions and divergent needs of divorcing couples invite a separatist approach in which advice and support are offered to each partner individually, instead of seeing them together. This separatist approach is encouraged by psychoanalytic theory, with its traditional focus on individual history and experience. A turning-point in the development of marital therapy in this country was reached when Dicks (1967) made his 'conceptual leap' across the limiting boundary of individual psychopathology to discover 'the interacting pair as the unit of perception and study' (p. 51). The conjoint interview which Dicks developed at the Tavistock Clinic in London from 1949 onwards was 'psychiatrically novel' at that time (p. 50). Nowadays, conjoint work with both partners on their marital problems is no longer controversial and it is gradually becoming more common with divorcing and divorced couples. Conjoint work during separation and divorce is challenging and problematic, yet it may help family members negotiate difficult transitions and reduce some of the loss they suffer.

One of the problems of working with divorcing couples is that they rarely move through the divorce process at the same rate, especially as they usually start from different points at different times. It is not surprising therefore that they often ask for and receive separate rather than conjoint help from professional and voluntary helpers. There may be sound reasons for working with one partner only but practice in both statutory and voluntary agencies suggests that conjoint work with separated or divorcing couples may be avoided for a number of reasons. The worker may identify consciously or unconsciously with one partner's position and feel disinclined to engage with the other partner. It is also very natural to fear losing control of a difficult meeting and to doubt whether it will achieve useful results. These psychological obstacles may be rationalised by the worker in terms of the insuperable practical difficulties of arranging joint appointments with both partners or ex-partners, especially if they no longer live in the same area. Proposing a joint or family meeting in a hesitant or half-hearted manner may also be a way of increasing the couple's resistance to the suggestion, justifying the worker's hidden reluctance to see them together.

Closer analysis of convening strategies may reveal that professionals sometimes use precisely those strategies which are least likely to engage both partners or ex-partners, despite a professed intention to reach them both. It is worth bearing in mind that there are not usually many difficulties in moving from an initial joint appointment to subsequent separate ones, if separate appointments are needed, whereas it may be more difficult to engage both partners after starting to work with one of them. Social workers should therefore be particularly cautious about engaging with one part of a disordered family system without paying sufficient attention to the system as a whole.

Interrelated dimensions of divorce

One of the first writers to conceptualise divorce as a complex psycho-social as well as legal process was Bohannan (1970), who identified six dimensions or 'stations' of the divorce experience: emotional, legal, economic, parental, community and psychic (psychological). Divorcing couples may be faced with problems in all these areas at the same time and conflict can spread quickly from one area to another. Conversely, agreement and co-operation in one area may encourage co-operation in other areas. There is however little multi-disciplinary help available which addresses all these areas at once. In a possibly unique multi-disciplinary project in the Netherlands, a counsellor, a child psychologist, a lawyer and a financial adviser work together in a divorce counselling bureau (McGillavry and Bijkerk, 1986). Divorcing individuals and couples can ask to see one or more of these specialists, who work separately and as co-workers in joint appointments. There is no comparable multi-disciplinary agency in Britain, apart from one or two family conciliation services in which a lawyer-mediator co-works with a mediator trained in social work and/or counselling. Some interdisciplinary knowledge is essential for effective work with families during separation or divorce. The references in each of the following sections are intended to act as signposts to more extensive treatments of the subjects concerned, since there is not space for detailed exploration of them here.

The emotional divorce

An emotional divorce may take place long before a couple separates physically. Alternatively, it may remain incomplete long after the legal divorce has been finalised. Pincus (1976), Morley (1982) and others have suggested that emotional closeness and distance in marriage may be simultaneously desired and feared. Some couples cannot grant each other the intimacy and space which they both need in varying degrees at different times, and these problems can lead to permanent estrangement. Bohannan (1970) suggests that inability to tolerate growth and change in one's partner causes an emotional divorce, whether there is a legal divorce or not. If the marriage fails to meet the needs of either partner, dissatisfaction may be suppressed but very often the partners blame each other in one way or another. They may gradually drift apart, perhaps finding compensation in other relationships or activities. For some of them, the legal divorce is merely a formality which confirms an existing and accepted separation and professional help may be needed only to deal with legal and financial technicalities. Some young couples part without ever becoming deeply attached to each other, while some older couples experience a gradual shrivelling of warmth and affection in which the other's presence becomes more of an irritant than a comfort.

This pattern of mutual disengagement does not seem to be typical, however. Very often, one partner tries to end the relationship while the other struggles to hold on to it. Kressel and Deutsch (1977) found that conflict over the ending of the marriage was associated with disputes on other issues and with poor post-divorce adjustment. 'The single most frequently cited predictor of a difficult divorce was one spouse's eagerness to end the marriage, coupled with reluctance to do so on the part of the spouse' (p. 423). If one spouse feels rejected by the other, he or she may react in various ways, many of which are counter-productive. Denying that the marriage is over keeps the conflict going, since even a bitter fight may be preferable to letting the partner go. The one who leaves may also behave erratically in ways that suggest some doubts about ending the relationship permanently. This ambivalence may entangle not only the divorced couple themselves but also their children, new partners, friends and would-be helpers in a sticky web of confused messages, misunderstandings and bitter accusations. Those who try to help an enmeshed couple achieve an emotional divorce may find that instead of achieving their aim they are sucked into the conflict and used as a means of keeping it going.

Between the two extremes of enmeshment and emotional disengagement there is a continuum of involvement between divorced couples which varies in frequency and intensity. Much of the literature on divorce focuses on the loss that is entailed, ignoring the extent to which many divorced couples retain or reconstruct relationships with each other which have enduring positive value for them and for their children. Recent studies in the Netherlands and the United States (ed. Cseh-Szombathy, 1985) show great variation in the way couples relate to each other after their divorce. Friendly and co-operative post-divorce relationships seem to be increasingly common among young couples and among the more highly educated (Weeda, 1985). As social workers tend to see the most problematic and intractable cases, it is important to keep some sense of perspective. Our optimism can help parents when they feel close to despair.

The legal divorce

The Divorce Reform Act in 1969 introduced the concept of the irretrievable breakdown of marriage as the sole ground for divorce in England and Wales. The new law made it possible for petitioners to obtain a divorce on the no-fault ground of two years' separation with the respondent's consent, and it was hoped that this more civilised approach would reduce the number of acrimonious divorces based on a 'matrimonial offence'. However, only 22 per cent of divorces in 1985 were based on two years' separation with consent, whereas 40 per cent were based on the respondent's 'unreasonable behaviour' and 30 per cent on adultery. Researchers at Oxford (Eekelaar and Maclean, 1983) found that parents in 'unreasonable behaviour' divorces were much more likely to fight over their children than in divorces based on adultery or separation. Most 'behaviour'petitions (virtually nine out of ten) are filed by wives. A husband who feels wrongfully accused may react either by disappearing altogether or by fighting over the children, money and the home – issues for which legal aid is more easily obtained than for the divorce itself. By insisting that certain 'facts' must be proved to demonstrate irretrievable breakdown, the present law still encourages petitioners to exaggerate or fabricate evidence against their former partner. In a survey of over 300 divorced people conducted by a market research company on behalf of *Woman* magazine (1982), 27 per cent of those interviewed admitted basing their petition on untrue 'facts' in order to obtain a quick divorce. If divorce is unacceptable to the petitioner, perhaps for religious reasons, a judicial separation may be sought instead but similar fault-based evidence is often used in judicial separation proceedings, rather than the no-fault ground of two years' separation.

The 1969 Act opened the floodgates to divorce on a massive scale, without providing procedures and special services to help divorcing couples reach well-considered and constructive decisions, especially where their children are concerned. In the absence of any national policy or provision, local initiatives have been taken in many areas to set up conciliation schemes (see Chapter 5) and many solicitors are adopting a more conciliatory approach. In December 1982 a group of solicitors formed the Solicitors' Family Law Association with a Code of Practice designed to encourage negotiated settlements in divorce rather than hostile litigation (*Family Law* 14, 1984, pp. 156–7). By the summer of 1986, about 1000 family solicitors had joined the Association. The courts, too, are encouraging a conciliatory approach but changes have been made in an ad hoc, piecemeal fashion without the fundamental overhaul that is needed. Comprehensive reform of divorce and family law is essential. Many professionals anxious to achieve some action by central government are now joining together in the campaign for a unified family court (see Chapter 7).

The economic divorce

For most families, divorce brings or aggravates financial hardship and divorcing couples are much more likely to fight over money than over their children. In 1981, 62 per cent of legal aid certificates in divorce and other matrimonial cases were for maintenance proceedings, compared with 15 per cent for contested custody and access proceedings and 7 per cent concerning the divorce itself (Lord Chancellor's Advisory Committee, 1983, para. 89). Public campaigns as well as private battles are waged over the rights and wrongs of financial support after divorce, but in the vast majority of cases the amount of maintenance ordered by the courts does not nearly cover the real cost of bringing up children. Maclean and Eekelaar (1983) found that the total maintenance paid to divorced mothers with dependent children was below £10 per week in half the cases, between £10 and £20 in a quarter and over £20 in the remaining quarter. Gibson (1982) showed likewise that only a small minority of women with maintenance orders enforceable in the magistrates' courts were receiving realistic maintenance on a regular basis.

Divorce accentuates existing economic divisions in society, plunging already poor households into greater poverty (Davis, Macleod and Murch, 1983b). The courts are supposed to give priority to children's needs but as Levin (1984) says, little effort is expended on translating this rhetoric into reality. The economic position of children in divorce will not be improved significantly by tinkering with the private law of maintenance. More could be done by improving state benefits, employment opportunities and daycare facilities for working parents and by tax reforms (Smart, 1984). As poverty is almost certainly the most acute problem faced by single parents, closely followed by housing problems, it is essential that social workers are able to give adequate welfare rights advice as well as referring clients to specialist sources of advice and help.

The parental divorce

Divorce ends marriage, not parenthood, but many couples effectively divorce each other as parents as well as ending their marriage. The option of joint custody may not even be considered, access may be a source of constant acrimony, if it takes place at all. Non-custodial parents (the term itself is demeaning) tend to feel disqualified and redundant. If access is confined to a few hours per month or even less, their relationship with the children easily becomes tenuous and artificial and may gradually dwindle away. Research evidence from England, Wales and Scotland shows that at least 25 to 30 per cent of children lose touch with one parent very soon after the separation (Mitchell, 1985), while in Northern Ireland, the absent parent is likely to lose touch with the children in about half of all divorces involving children (McCoy and

Nelson, 1983). Some fathers believe the children will settle down better if they stop visiting them, perhaps because they themselves find short visits and repeated goodbyes unbearably painful. It can be easier to play the role of a martyred parent who gives up attempts to see the children than to struggle to maintain a relationship with them in the face of the other parent's hostility, and feigned or sometimes genuine indifference from the children themselves.

Some mothers feel secure only if they manage to cut themselves off from their former partner, particularly where there has been violence. A complete break may nonetheless leave some of them with feelings of unresolved grief and anger which may complicate subsequent relationships. A father who feels pushed out of the family is less likely to pay maintenance for his children and if access is withheld until maintenance is paid, the result may be a deadlock with no maintenance and no access. This 'unclean break' is usually very damaging for the children, except in cases where the absent parent has been violent to them or is deeply disturbed. As social work intervention in divorce is often focused on custody and access problems, ways of helping families resolve these problems form one of the main subjects of this book.

The community divorce

Ten years ago, Hart (1976) found that 80 per cent of the divorced people in her study considered loneliness their most pressing problem. Today, material deprivation probably causes as much misery as the psychological effects of separation. In Hart's study, half the women and one-third of the men had to find new accommodation after separating. The disruption of moving away from a familiar environment, neighbours and friends increases personal trauma for adults and children, and this affects custodial parents and their children much more often than is commonly supposed. Southwell (1985) found in a study in a large northern city that nearly half the children had to leave the family home. either because it was sold or because it was occupied by the non-custodial parent. Mitchell (1985) found likewise that nearly a quarter of the children in her Scottish sample had moved home three or four times, one of them five times and one girl more times than she could remember. The practical problems and anxieties of finding new accommodation and new schools for the children are accentuated if parents lose the very neighbours and friends who might have provided support. Single parents cannot usually afford a baby-sitter and parents who live alone, without their children, may feel too depressed to pursue new interests or relationships (Ambrose, Harper and Pemberton, 1983).

When a marriage breaks up, one partner often seeks refuge with his or her parents who may readily offer the practical help and support they desperately need (Mitchell, 1981; Brannen and Collard, 1982). Many grandparents, however, have neither room nor inclination to house grown-up offspring and from the separated parent's point of view, renewed dependence on their own parents involves a loss of adult status and self-esteem. Hart (1976) found that couples who had relied on joint friendships during their marriage felt particularly isolated after their separation. Many avoided the company of former friends and acquaintances because they feared being wounded by their gossip or criticism. They were particularly wary of confiding in anyone who was also in touch with their former partner, feeling inhibited by loyalty to their husband or wife or by fear of confidences being passed on by untrustworthy friends. Those who experienced a sharp drop in living standards following their separation were understandably reluctant to play the part of poor relation and depend on other people's generosity. A separated person tends to feel the odd one out on social occasions where most people have partners. Married couples' conversations and interests differ from single parents' preoccupations and may be very upsetting to them, reminding them of what they have lost.

One of the tasks which may take years to accomplish after separation or divorce is the gradual rebuilding of a social network. Social workers can help separated parents by understanding these difficulties and providing information about daycare facilities and groups run by local voluntary organisations.

Psychological divorce

Individuals who remain devastated by the loss of their partner may not be able to move forward into new relationships and activities. They may need extensive therapeutic help to repair their damaged self-esteem and become independent. Bohannan (1970, p. 488) defined psychological divorce as 'the separation of self from the personality and influence of the ex-spouse'. He recognised that learning to live without depending on someone else can be extremely difficult. It involves knowing and valuing oneself as an independent human being and managing to be self-sufficient, with or without support from relatives, friends and colleagues. For the divorced, it involves learning to cope with practical matters for which the former partner previously took responsibility, such as paying bills or doing the laundry. Divorced men tend to lead more erratic and chaotic lives than married men, sleeping less and catering for themselves only with difficulty (Kitson and Sussman, 1977). Divorced women, too, are liable to feel disorientated and many seek medical help for depression and eating and sleep problems, especially in the early stages of separation (Chester, 1971). Although some people may grasp eagerly at the independence they previously lacked, many experience a deep fear of being totally alone. This fear, and the social and financial problems that may accompany it, often pushes people into new relationships and remarriage before they have extricated themselves sufficiently from the previous relationship. Burgoyne and Clark (1984) found in their study of stepfamilies in Sheffield that the ending of one relationship often overlapped with the beginning of another and that this could be very problematic and stressful for all concerned.

The main task in psychological divorce is therefore to confront and master the problem of personal autonomy. This involves taking full responsibility for one's own decisions and mistakes and no longer being able to blame one's partner (or other people) when things go wrong. Self-esteem tends to be measured in terms of satisfactory relationships with others (Weiss, 1975) and divorce may shatter the sense of identity and belonging, especially for those who married to avoid becoming fully independent. Bohannan (1970) believes that the strongest argument against teenage marriage or hasty remarriage is that individuals exchange one form of dependence for another, without becoming self-reliant. Although social workers cannot prevent people jumping hastily from one relationship to the next, they may help some of them to look more carefully where they are going, and perhaps slow the pace of change.

Divorce and bereavement

The loss of a partner through divorce has often been compared to loss through death (Parkes, 1972). The bereavement which accompanies divorce may result in prolonged depression and 'anomie' in which life seems pointless and everyday tasks become drained of meaning (Hart, 1976). Kitson and colleagues (1980) found many similarities in the feelings of divorcees and widows, though the knowledge that their partner left of his own free will leaves some divorcees more bitter and humiliated than widows generally do. Divorcees tend to be considerably younger than widows and they are therefore more likely to remarry, but adjustment in both groups is complicated where there are strong feelings of anger, rejection or guilt.

On the positive side, death and divorce can bring release from unhappy or restrictive relationships, freeing individuals to build a new life either on their own or with a new partner. The need to mourn is however better understood and provided for in relation to death than in divorce. The anger which is an expected response in divorce may be maintained as a defence against grief, blocking a necessary process of mourning. The partner who chose to leave may also feel prevented from grieving, in case an expression of regret is misinterpreted as a desire for reconciliation. Incomplete mourning delays personal adjustment and may cause major difficulties in subsequent relationships.

The pressures on social workers are such that they can rarely work with people through the months and years in which they may continue to mourn the loss of their marriage or living-together relationship. Divorce experience courses (Morley, 1985; Read, 1985), although very short, may help people as they struggle through the mourning process. These courses are now being run in many parts of the country to offer information and shared insights on divorce, with the possibility of continued support and friendships between course members after the course ends. Social workers, welfare officers, marriage counsellors and conciliators often come together to run these courses, generally finding these joint ventures a positive counterbalance to the strains of their everyday work.

Joint decisions in divorce

Divorce and separation are much less traumatic for children and their parents if the parents are able to take joint decisions as far as possible. Hart (1976) contrasted active and passive roles in the process of separation and divorce and found that those who felt 'acted against' had much more difficulty adjusting than those who initiated the break-up. Initiators and recipients of divorce may be poles apart from each other, yet there are decisions and tasks which need to be addressed jointly if possible, particularly if they have children. Addressing these decisions and tasks jointly instead of unilaterally can help bridge the gulf between them, but many couples are unable to communicate constructively in the crises of separation, especially where there has been a long history of failed communication in their relationship. They need help to listen to each other, to express and understand each other's concerns and to work out possible ways of coping. Some couples may then recognise the positive parts of their previous life together as well as its disappointments and may then feel more motivated to work together as parents, despite their personal distress.

Social workers can help by providing a bridge, both emotionally and practically, where members of divided families can meet each other on neutral territory to talk about their problems and concerns. This bridge may help families negotiate difficult transitions and reach firmer ground. As far as social workers themselves are concerned, it represents a practical, pragmatic response to demands that often seem unmanageable. The demand for social work services greatly exceeds the time available, and the focus of this book is on brief but carefully structured work with couples and families rather than on exhaustive (and exhausting) work with individuals on a one-to-one basis.

2

The Crisis of Separation

Marriage breakdown, divorce and crisis theory

Over the last twenty years, research studies and clinical work have made us much more aware of the effects of cumulative stress on individuals and families. We have been alerted particularly to the stress that accompanies transitions in the family life-cycle, such as children being born or leaving home, and the effect this can have on fragile marriages (Carter and McGoldrick, 1980; Clulow, 1982). Terkelson (1980) distinguished 'normative' events in family life from 'paranormative' events, such as illness, disability and unemployment. The divorce rate for the unemployed is exceptionally high and although the incidence of divorce decreases among longer-married couples, even unemployed husbands in their fifties show an extremely high rate of divorce (Haskey, 1984). A causal relationship between unemployment and divorce has not been proven but the poverty and loss of status associated with unemployment inevitably puts enormous strain on the unemployed and their families. Research suggests that unemployed men are more than twice as likely to commit suicide and 80 per cent more likely to have a fatal accident, compared with employed men of the same age (Nuffield Centre, 1984).

Divorce, like unemployment, tends to be inversely correlated with social class, with unskilled manual workers (socio-economic group 5) four times more likely to divorce than men in socio-economic group 1 (Haskey, 1984). Occupations involving long or frequent absences from home, such as the armed forces and some personal service occupations, also carry high risks of divorce. Although one in twenty divorces in 1979 involved couples who had been married over thirty years (Rimmer, 1982), divorce is occurring within shorter durations of marriage, especially for couples marrying in their teens. Divorce offers an escape from intolerable stress but many people are unprepared for the further stress involved in the divorce process itself. If they take major decisions hastily, without considering or even understanding the alternatives available, they may experience a state of severe crisis and their readjustment may be slow and painful.

Writers on crisis theory (Parad and Caplan, 1965; Rapoport, 1965; Caplan, 1985) have suggested that crisis generally involves:

(a) a stressful event or situation to which no immediate solution can be found,
(b) a major threat to identity and routine reviving unresolved problems from both the near and distant past, and
(c) reactions forming a recognisable pattern of disorganisation and distress, starting with an acute phase which typically lasts around six to eight weeks.

The Chinese character for crisis denotes both 'danger' and 'opportunity', suggesting that although the risks are very high for individuals who feel overwhelmed and unsupported, crisis can lead to positive change and growth, possibly resulting in higher levels of functioning than before the crisis occurred. This positive approach to crisis implies that the outcome depends more on how it is handled than on the precipitating event itself. Brannen and Collard (1982) found in their study of troubled marriages that the great majority of couples had recently experienced at least one major critical event, problem or dissatisfaction before the problems in their marriage came to a head. Although these triggering events or problems did not necessarily cause the marriage to break down, they were likely to have depleted the emotional resources of one or both partners and thus increased the risk of a breakdown occurring. Brannen and Collard went on to hypothesise that when critical events and problems are experienced by couples whose relationship is already strained, they are likely to have much greater impact on couples who depend exclusively on each other. These couples typically have little support from relatives and friends but often avoid seeking professional help until the crisis reaches unmanageable levels. Lindemann (1965) pointed out that the timing of professional intervention in crisis situations is very important and that early intervention can forestall later, more serious consequences. Resistance to outside intervention is often lower in the early stages of crisis and as Rapoport (1965) observed, 'the degree of activity of the helping person does not have to be high. A little help, *rationally directed, and purposefully focused at a strategic time* (italics supplied) is more effective than more extensive help given at a period of less emotional accessibility' (p. 30).

In severe marital crisis, one or both partners may turn to a social work agency for help, despite their reluctance to disclose personal problems to outsiders who might not be sympathetic or trustworthy. The agency's response calls for particularly careful assessment at the intake stage, as the opportunity for strategic intervention is easily missed. This initial assessment needs to take account of salient questions such as who is the client, how urgent the situation seems to be and whether legal advice is needed. The conflicts of family break-up can involve high risks of physical violence, murder and suicide, as tragic stories in the press remind us every day. Social workers may need to refer people for emergency medical help and they should have enough grasp of the law to give accurate preliminary advice. For example, a parent who decides to leave the children temporarily with the other parent while looking for somewhere else to live needs to be aware of the risk of losing custody of the children.

Who is the client?

Whitaker and Miller (1969) warn that 'psychotherapeutic intervention on one side or another in a marriage, when divorce is being considered, may serve to destroy the possibility of reconciliation. Despite the therapist's efforts to remain neutral, he inevitably finds himself thrust into the role of catalyst, judge or alternative mate' (p. 57). Steinberg

(1980) agrees that it may be a tactical blunder to respond to the help-seeking partner without seeking to engage the other partner at the outset. 'When divorce threatens, it has been my experience that individual therapy is more likely to polarise the marital dyad and increase the possibility of an adversarial dissolution' (p. 261).

There are a number of reasons for offering help to both partners equally rather than to one alone, including the following:

(a) Major decisions are often taken in crisis situations on the basis of misunderstandings or because of failed or wholly negative communications. Joint discussion with both partners may enable them not only to talk to each other, but more importantly, to listen to each other. Information is a fundamental ingredient of decision-making, and the quality of decisions depends to a large extent on the capacity to absorb and process information. Couples who lack basic communication skills may need help to focus their discussions and manage their anger and fear, while they identify and weigh up alternative courses of action. Although neither partner may be prepared to change tack, and potentially explosive information or feelings may still be concealed, conjoint discussion with them both may clarify their situation more effectively than separate interviews with each partner alone.

(b) A fresh possibility may emerge in discussions with both partners which had not previously occurred to either of them as a viable way forward.

(c) Many unhappy couples feel deeply ambivalent about each other and find it very hard to come to terms with this ambivalence. Their uncertainty and fear of loss may be so unbearable that separation may seem preferable, yet their unresolved attachment may result in repeated separations and in confused and contradictory verbal and non-verbal messages. Conjoint work may enable them to acknowledge their ambivalent feelings and give each other clearer messages, especially if the worker helps normalise these mixed feelings so that they become more manageable. If they are not dealt with, they may continue to cause problems over a long period and may be imported into new relationships. Stepfamilies are often upset by the intrusion of one parent's former partner. The stability of second marriages and stepfamilies may depend on whether a previous marriage or relationship ended in an unambiguous way for both partners, leaving them free to make new relationships.

(d) Apart from their cathartic function in ventilating anger and frustration, these joint discussions can demonstrate that neither partner has enlisted the worker or agency as a personal ally. This is important, since couples in conflict with each other often try to recruit other more powerful systems to defeat each other's support-system. The worker's impartiality may reassure them that they both have valid concerns which merit equal attention from helping agencies.

(e) Seeing both partners together helps workers assess with them both whether their difficulties are due to conflicting needs, communication problems, stresses in the wider family system or all these factors combined. Possible sources of help can then be considered with them both and a plan may be worked out which both are willing to try, at least temporarily. A short or longer-term contract may be made for further work on the problems that have been identified, or referral to another agency may be indicated. Workers need to take great care in the initial stage of work to clarify expectations and objectives, especially where the partners come with different agendas. Accepting their clash of interests and allotting equal time to each partner's agenda may enable them to engage in further conjoint work.

Conjoint interviews in situations of domestic violence?

The incidence of domestic violence is extremely high, especially in the crisis of actual or threatened separation, but much of it goes unreported (Pahl, 1985). If a battered woman contacts a social worker, the worker may not think it appropriate to see both partners together, since the woman may be afraid to talk in the presence of the man who has assaulted her. Conjoint interviews are certainly undesirable if the man's domination is allowed to continue and the woman is put under further pressure to continue the relationship, regardless of the risks or stress she is enduring. On the other hand, if sufficient protection and support can be provided, the woman may become more, not less, able to express her needs and concerns. If co-working is a possibility (see Chapter 5), this should be considered, as two or more workers may offer more protection and support to both partners than a single worker is able to provide.

A social worker with ten years' experience in a social services area office dealing with many different kinds of family crisis has observed that 'confidence is the key of success in crisis intervention and actual experience is the most effective means of acquiring confidence' (O'Hagan, 1984, p. 174). Confidence is liable to vanish, however, when angry voices are raised and tempers begin to boil over. Moore (1982) has written graphically that 'contact with violence produces a turmoil of conflicting and confusing feelings, which fixes the worker into a petrified stance, like a rabbit caught at night in the headlights of a car: impotent, with that particular impotence which brings about its own demise' (p. 18). Workers who wonder despairingly if they are expected to acquire confidence through a process of trial and terror may be helped by short training courses which include a substantial amount of role-play and video. Although social work students acting in role-plays may not express the raw emotion of real life and role-plays cannot reproduce the anarchy and anguish of family crisis, a lot can be learnt none the less. This learning is of limited value if techniques are then applied by the book: the objective should be to encourage the selection of appropriate strategies and the invention of new ones. Training needs to be combined with practical experience, supervision and good team support so that workers develop confidence in taking charge of conjoint or family meetings and keeping discussions under sufficient control. A worker who takes a judgemental position, possibly through anxiety, loses his or her manoeuvrability and may even provoke violence from a family member who feels misunderstood and blamed.

A non-partisan stance is important in the first stage of work, while initial assessments are being made. Workers then have a basis for deciding whether to offer individual support to one partner or to continue with neutral help to both. In any case, neutrality towards both partners should not be seen as neutrality towards the violence itself. Violent behaviour needs to be challenged and even the violent partner may welcome this. A person who has never lost control before may be feeling deeply ashamed and terrified of further loss of control. He or she may become able to use words instead of physical violence if a channel of communication is opened up for the desperation and fear which may underlie the violence.

The structure of conjoint meetings with both partners (location and length of appointments, arrangements for reception and seating and the focus of discussion) needs careful planning. If a woman fears meeting her partner, it is important to understand her fears. She may dread being left alone with him in the waiting-room, being pressed to give in to his demands, being followed afterwards, or all these things. A slightly earlier time of arrival can enable her to be settled in the interview room without coming face to face with him on the doorstep and in some cases it may be agreed beforehand that her husband or partner will stay behind for an extra twenty minutes or so, so that she can leave the building without fear of being followed. This can be arranged without forming an alliance with her if the worker emphasises that neither partner has been prejudged on the basis of unchecked complaints from the other.

Confidentiality

Confidentiality is an important issue when violence or other abuse is complained of and social workers need to be explicit with their clients about the degree of confidentiality they can provide. Researchers at Bristol University (Borkowski, Murch and Walker, 1983) found in their study of domestic violence that distressed women were very conscious of confidentiality and this often determined which agency they contacted. Many sought private consultations with their doctor or solicitor and some went to a refuge because it offered total secrecy. Empirical evidence suggests that many people contact the Citizens' Advice Bureau because it offers information and advice without inquiring too closely into their personal lives. Parents who are separating tend to feel very vulnerable and they may regard statutory welfare agencies with fear and mistrust. Suddenly even the parenting of their children comes under scrutiny, causing perfectly competent parents to develop irrational fears of their children being taken into care. Even if a parent does not inquire about the extent of the confidentiality provided by social workers, he or she should be told whether the discussions will be reportable to anyone, in any circumstances. It is essential to mention possible exceptions to the normal rules of confidentiality, of which child abuse is an obvious example. Social workers need to explain their responsibilities and statutory powers in a clear but non-accusatory manner so that clients appreciate from the outset how the information they give might be handled. This does not appear to deter them from explaining that a child is or may be at risk. On the contrary, social workers who give clear explanations of their objectives and responsibilities may be accepted as more trustworthy than those who fudge awkward questions of confidentiality. The following case illustrates the importance of engaging and convening both parents *before* beginning to understand and respond to their problems.

Case study – the Smith family

June Smith telephoned a social worker on her solicitor's advice, explaining that she had left her husband, Roy, two days previously and that she was now in a refuge. Her two children, aged six and eight, were with her but as she had not had time to pack their clothes and favourite toys they were missing many things and could not understand why they could not go home to get them. June said she was starting divorce proceedings and in the meantime she wanted the social worker to go to the house and collect the things she needed for the children, or alternatively, her husband could be asked to bring them to the social worker's office. There had apparently been several incidents in which he had hit her, on one occasion in front of the children, and from her initial account there seemed little doubt that the court would grant her a divorce, sole custody of the children and the occupation of the matrimonial home. On the face of it, the 'best interests of the child' principle appeared to justify supporting June and helping her provide a secure and stable home for the children.

The social worker said she understood the urgency of June's position and asked what she had told the children about seeing their father. She replied they did not seem to be missing him in the least and although they ought to see him sometime, she did not see how, as she was not prepared to take them anywhere to meet him. She knew he would only use a meeting to put pressure on her to have him back. The worker suggested that there were urgent matters including financial arrangements, access for the children and the occupation of the family home which might be solved more easily if Roy was willing to co-operate with her instead of fighting her every inch of the way. June thought any co-operation from him was most unlikely but agreed to come to a joint meeting to see if any of these practical problems could be resolved. She agreed to come on three conditions: first, that the worker would guarantee not to pass on her address to Roy; secondly, that there would be no discussion at all about reconciliation, as she was not willing to consider it; and thirdly, that Roy would stay behind at the office so that she could leave safely without fear that he would follow her and find out where she was living.

In making the first approach to Roy, the worker was aware that her contact with June and her knowledge of June's whereabouts might give the impression that she was on June's side. He might refuse to come to any meeting if he believed she had already formed a bad opinion of him and that she was supporting 'the woman and kids'. If he thought the world was against him, he might not only refuse to co-operate but could make things even worse for June and the children. Somehow, Roy needed to be persuaded that the worker had not prejudged the situation on the basis of June's version of events and that she was concerned to help the whole family, if possible. She decided to write to him, rather than telephoning or calling to see him. A phone call or home visit would take him by surprise and might make him more suspicious, whereas he would have more time to think about the contents of a letter before deciding what to do about it. The worker explained in her letter that following the phone call from June she was concerned to understand how he (Roy) saw the situation. She expressed concern about the upset the children must be feeling and asked Roy if he would telephone as soon as possible, mentioning times when she would be available.

Roy phoned at the first opportunity, sounding upset and somewhat aggressive but willing to accept the appointment. The worker explained to him that June was not willing to discuss coming home and that the only way of persuading her to meet him at all was to promise her that the discussion would be limited to urgent questions concerning the children. Although Roy was desperate to talk about the recent incident and to justify his own behaviour by blaming June, he accepted the conditions for the meeting and agreed to stick to them. Both he and June turned up for their appointment the following day, Roy carrying several bags of clothes and toys for the children and a bunch of flowers for June. Her face stiffened when she saw the flowers but nothing was said about them and she seemed reassured that the worker was keeping to the agreed agenda. Some immediate questions concerning the children were sorted out in this very stressful meeting, leaving major questions still in the air about the ending of the marriage and the occupation of the family home. However, the realisation that some form of co-operation was possible in relation to the children led to further meetings, including a meeting the following week when June brought the children to see Roy, again on the understanding that this in no way implied a willingness on her part to consider reconciliation. Their daughter, Sharon, climbed on Roy's knee as soon as she saw him and both children showed that they were very attached to their father. This direct evidence contradicted June's earlier statement that they did not miss him in the least.

The outcome of further discussions with this couple was a voluntary undertaking by Roy to leave the matrimonial home by a certain date and move to live with his father. Although this could be seen as a surrender on his part which might have left him very bitter or profoundly depressed, his sense of loss was lessened by being directly involved in decisions about his marriage and family and by agreements on joint custody and regular access to the children.

Strategies of crisis intervention

The main strategies of crisis intervention used with this family were as follows:

1. Considerable care was taken at the outset to establish a working alliance with both parents, although it would have been much easier to offer support and assistance to June and the children and the facts as initially presented would have justified doing so. When June and Roy came to the first meeting, looking very tense and hostile, the worker greeted them warmly and kept equal eye contact with them as they talked. She addressed them directly and was careful not to refer to either of them in the third person.

2. Care was also taken to negotiate an agenda for the first meeting that both parents could accept and then to structure the meeting so that this agenda was adhered to.

3. The high level of emotion at the first meeting was contained in a number of ways: (a) by arranging the chairs in a triangular pattern, angled towards the centre, so that June and Roy did not confront each other across the worker and she could look at both of them at the same time; (b) by setting rules that each of them would have an equal opportunity to speak and neither would be permitted to interrupt the other; (c) by emphasising that although they might be deeply divided as man and wife, they were still parents of their children and had joint responsibility to minimise their distress; and (d) by setting precise time-boundaries which reserved the last quarter of an hour for summarising and confirming the next steps to be taken.

4. The focus was kept on the here and now. This did not mean that the past was ignored as the strong feelings brought to the discussions were recognised. But instead of

urging Roy and June to reach agreement on major issues, which would have increased their anxiety and conflict, the worker commented that it would not be reasonable to expect them to settle such difficult and complicated questions in a short time. By recognising the scale of the problems and their conflicting objectives and perceptions, she helped lower the emotional temperature and prevent an explosion. It was agreed that they should first concentrate on the immediate questions which needed to be dealt with in the next seven days. This led to a task-centred approach in which priorities were identified, including June's need for financial support from Roy and his need to see the children. Access to the children was not offered as a *quid pro quo* in return for a voluntary maintenance payment, but both partners were encouraged to give some tangible evidence of co-operation. When the initial crisis was brought under some control, it became easier to consider the underlying problems. With both partners' consent, the worker contacted their solicitors, who gave helpful advice and prepared applications for consent orders.

Case study – the Brown family

In the following case, the initial crisis-point had passed long before the social worker became involved. These parents were firmly entrenched in fixed negative attitudes towards each other and the wife's main concern was to cut herself off from her husband completely. The more he demanded access to their child, the more barriers she set up to prevent any contact.

Alan and Marcia Brown were in their early twenties. Alan had been posted to West Germany with the army and after a year of frequent and often violent rows, Marcia had returned home to her parents in Somerset, together with their two-year old daughter, Jacqueline. She had left a note for Alan to tell him she was leaving him and not coming back. Alan obtained compassionate leave and followed Marcia back to England and at some point he managed to snatch Jacqueline. Marcia then applied for a custody order in the magistrates' court, as her divorce petition had not yet been filed, and she was awarded sole custody, care and control of Jacqueline. The question of Alan's access was adjourned for a welfare inquiry, to see whether contact with her father even at infrequent intervals would benefit Jacqueline and whether Alan might manage to handle the visits responsibly. A conjoint interview shortly after the court hearing indicated that:

1. Alan and Marcia had great difficulty in recognising and responding to Jacqueline's needs: they seemed to treat her merely as a pawn in their personal battle. Alan expressed regret about snatching her and undertook not to do so again, but Marcia was adamant that there should be no access and said she wanted nothing further to do with him.

2. Marcia complained that Alan was committed to the army rather than to her and she resented the army's control of their lives. She had felt very isolated in Germany and became depressed when Alan spent evenings drinking with his mates. The more she withdrew from him, the more heavily he drank, and he tended to become violent towards her after drinking. Marcia felt that the army had destroyed their marriage because Alan did not want to jeopardise his career and she could not face the long separations and frequent moves which life in the army would entail. Her parents, from whom she had never been separated before, had urged her to come home and offered her the emotional refuge she needed. She seemed relieved to sink back into the role of daughter in her parents' home and to let them manage her life much as the army ruled Alan's. The break-up of the marriage therefore needed to be seen in the context of two powerful systems which were acting like two magnets pulling Alan and Marcia in opposite directions. They were unable to take any joint decisions as parents partly because they were each treated as children by powerful parental or quasi-parental systems. One possibility was to work at this wider systems level by inviting Marcia's parents and a social worker from the army to come to a meeting with Alan and Marcia to talk about Alan's access to Jacqueline.

If some co-operation could be established between the two 'super-parent' systems, Alan and Marcia might feel they had permission to relate to each other as co-parents despite the ending of the marriage. This 'network' approach will be considered further in Chapter 7.

If the two cases which have been briefly referred to are compared in terms of Bohannan's (1970) dimensions of divorce (see Chapter 1), there are obvious differences, although both cases involved marital violence and both wives proceeded to divorce their husbands. Alan and Marcia were a young couple who treated their child as a possession instead of as a person with needs of her own. Unlike Roy and June, they were not able to separate their parental relationship from the marital one and communication between them was very volatile. They continued to fight over financial and legal issues, whereas Roy and June developed more co-operative attitudes towards each other once the level of crisis was contained. Early intervention in the first case helped arrest the downward spiral in which Roy and June had got caught. By offering them a safe and neutral forum for discussion, the opportunity to take stock of their alternatives and support in doing so, the worker helped them work out the basis for ending their marriage with as little trauma as possible, for themselves and their children. However, if the situation had been handled adversarially, Roy and June would probably have lost their ability and motivation to co-operate as parents and Roy might then have lost all contact with the children.

Understanding conflict patterns

We may be able to relate better to couples at different stages of separation if we can distinguish varying levels of conflict and recognise certain patterns, even though each situation is unique and we must avoid fitting families to preconceived theories. The following typology is rudimentary and the categories should not be seen as mutually exclusive. Some couples show more than one pattern of conflict at the same time and many move through time from one pattern to another. Nor can conflicts be described only in dyadic terms, since children and other adults may be closely involved too. Children's involvement in parental disputes will be discussed further in the next chapter and the role of new partners and step-parents will be considered in subsequent chapters. First impressions of the level and type of conflict between separating and divorcing couples can be misleading, but they at least offer a starting-point for planning how to work with them. Many situations of family breakup are so confused that it is hard to know whether the changes being sought are really wanted and how much change is realistically possible. The following simple typology may help gauge the amount of control that may be needed in structured discussions with both partners. Some couples may be able to work only on a very limited and practical agenda, whereas others may want to discuss much deeper problems in their relationships with each other and with their children.

1. *Semi-detached couples*
These couples may have drifted apart over a period of time and their separation may take place with relatively little overt conflict. There may be practical difficulties, however, and friction over access visits may indicate that the parents are still partly engaged with each other emotionally. Joint discussions may help them disentangle marital and parental roles and strengthen their co-operation as parents. Some parents respond relatively quickly to this approach and if they begin talking to each other in a more friendly way, the worker can intervene progressively less, leaving them to manage the discussion themselves. If new partners are involved on either side, it may be helpful to involve them too (see Chapter 6). Bringing people together to work on a clearly defined agenda for the future can be very productive in helping them put past conflicts behind them.

2. *Closed door conflict*
Some couples avoid direct confrontation by retreating behind closed doors, physically, psychologically or both. Their silence conveys rejection, anger, frustration and the withdrawal of love, although few words are spoken. There may also be unspoken messages of continuing attachment, deep

hurt and fear of abandonment. One partner may leave home or start divorce proceedings without warning. If major questions concerning the divorce, care of the children, financial matters and housing are shelved by a parent who is unprepared to deal with them, the family may endure prolonged uncertainty and insecurity. Children are often not told why the absent parent has left, nor if, when and how they will see him or her again. The pattern of silence and avoidance is thus passed on to the next generation. In some very unhappy and stressful situations, the partners withdraw from each other and one proceeds to divorce the other, typically for 'unreasonable behaviour', but both continue to live separately under the same roof. The tensions may be unbearable and vulnerable children may show their reactions in depression, delinquent behaviour or failure at school.

Wherever possible, these closed-door couples should be seen together but separate appointments may be needed initially to help them establish some trust in the worker before they can face the strain of talking with each other. The offer of a joint meeting may then be accepted, but the pace of work needs to be carefully adjusted to the amount of stress or movement each of them can cope with at one time: it may need to be very slow initially and the worker needs to be attentive to unexpressed and ambivalent feelings. Winnicott (1977) and Haynes (1982) have written about the importance of listening with a sensitive 'third ear' which hears feelings which may be too painful or alarming to express directly. Rather than putting direct questions to each partner, it is often helpful to ask one what he or she thinks the other may be wanting or feeling, and then to ask the second partner whether their position has been conveyed more or less accurately.

3. *The battle for power*
Individuals faced with a major loss in their lives may react by fighting for a dominant position in their divorce proceedings. The act of separation or divorce may itself be an attempt to reverse an imbalance of power in the family and this struggle may continue with new levers or weapons – such as playing on the other partner's guilt or their fear of censure from relatives

and community leaders, or by taking possession of the children, or by exploiting legal advantages in court (Mnookin and Kornhauser, 1979; Mnookin, 1984; Parkinson, 1986a).

Some of these couples may respond to structured conciliation techniques (see Chapter 5) in which issues are identified and an agenda drawn up which allots equal time to each partner's concerns. Time boundaries can be set for each issue on the agenda, so that it can be looked at carefully and systematically from each parent's point of view and from the children's position. It may be possible to identify some common ground and reach some degree of agreement, especially if conciliators select an issue that may be negotiable before moving on to more complex or emotive problems. Impossible demands need to be recognised as such and conciliators may need to set some ground-rules initially, such as not permitting either partner to interrupt the other.

4. *Tenacious clinging*
A very common pattern of conflict consists of one partner trying to push the other away, while the resistant partner struggles to cling on. The resistant partner's appeals may take the form of emotional blackmail, such as threats of suicide or physical injury, and these threats should not be disregarded as the risks may be high. Sometimes the partner who has left feels compelled to return but the attempt at reconciliation may be short-lived and the bereft partner may be left more hurt and angry than before.

Conjoint work with these couples may perpetuate rather than solve their problems, as the partner who has left may want a quick exit while the other one usually wants to prolong the contact as much as possible. The bereft partner usually needs much more time and help to come to terms with the separation and to face a future which may seem totally bleak and empty. Other sources of help should be considered, such as individual counselling and divorce experience courses (see Chapter 3), which help some grieving and bitter individuals assimilate some of their pain, drawing support from others who have been through a similar experience. If the rejected partner has no relatives or friends to turn to, he or she may accept contact with a local community group, especially if a member of the group is willing to visit the person at home initially. Members of Gingerbread and Families Need Fathers can be extremely helpful and supportive, having often endured similar distress themselves.

5. *Confrontation*
Many couples feel shocked and humiliated if they find themselves slapping or punching each other in a completely uncharacteristic way, though this is very common in the crisis of separation. If help is sought from a social worker or counsellor, firm intervention may be needed initially to prevent the violence escalating. Appointments may need to be spaced only a few days apart, with friendly but firm instructions to both partners to avoid 'winding each other up' in between appointments. Some couples accept directive advice of this nature, understanding that they are temporarily dependent on external control – over the structure of their discussions but not the outcome – until they can regain their own control. If they are encouraged to focus as parents on issues concerning the children, this often helps them maintain their normal parenting capacity despite the emotional pressures of separating.

6. *Enmeshed conflict*
Kressel and colleagues (1980) used the term 'enmeshed' to describe couples who seem to have a strong emotional investment in keeping their fight going. They are very difficult to help, and brief social work intervention is unlikely to produce the fundamental improvement that may be hoped for. It may be useful none the less to focus on immediate practical matters, identifying the alternatives available and doing some reality-testing to see how far the consequences have been thought through. If there is some motivation from the couple to manage their conflict better, practical task-setting (Reid and Epstein, 1972) may be useful, such as asking each of them to suggest a manageable task that the other partner can be requested to undertake.

Couples who fall into Wallerstein and Kelly's (1980) category of 'embittered-chaotic' couples (p. 28) may actually need their anger to keep a grip on themselves and ward off the fear of total annihilation. Raging tirades can have a galvanising, organising function for individuals who are close to despair, but the force of their anger and desperation may make it very difficult to work with both partners. They may postpone decisions about their children in order to continue their battle and it may be helpful to reframe their conflict rather than trying to end it (see Chapter 5), since a dominant characteristic of these couples is their resistance to solutions being found. They can cause extreme frustration or depression in those who try to help them. Co-working may be helpful in these particularly difficult situations and in some cases adjudication by the court will be necessary in the interests of the children. Referral for longer-term, supportive counselling and/or a community-based support group may be acceptable to one or both partners.

7. *Domestic violence*
Where one partner has made repeated assaults on the other, it is important to find out whether both partners acknowledge the violence and whether the victim wants to end the relationship or only the violence. Sometimes alcohol or other substance abuse is a factor and the violent partner may accept treatment under the ultimatum from the other that the violence must stop completely, if the relationship is to continue. Some couples manage to speak more clearly and rationally to each other in the presence of one or more neutral helpers but it is essential to check whether urgent action is needed to protect the woman and the children, if they are also at risk.

Many women who suffer violence in the home are very uncertain what action they can and should take. Unfortunately the social work response to these situations often seems to be both muddled and inadequate. Pahl (1985) found in her study of battered women that the most helpful social workers were those who were able to give accurate information about emergency accommodation, social security and relevant legislation. Legal advice from a solicitor may be needed urgently, but researchers in Bristol (Borkowski, Murch and Walker, 1983) found that social workers' knowledge of the law and legal services was weak. Only 26 per cent were well informed about the law relating to domestic violence, compared with 68 per cent who said they had a little knowledge. Many of those who felt they were well informed were vague about injunctions and none mentioned the power of arrest provision.

Maynard (1985) and colleagues investigated what social workers in a northern town actually did in terms of offering advice and help to battered women. In a random sample of 103 current social work case files they found that 34 contained direct references to domestic violence. These cases involved serious physical assaults, sometimes with offensive weapons and often in conjunction with threats and warnings which meant that at least some of these women were living in a permanent state of intimidation and fear. The researchers concluded that 'for the vast majority of women the files indicate that nothing was done to immediately relieve the situation' (p. 129). In the minority of cases in which some action was taken, two women were placed in a psychiatric hospital and three couples were referred to marriage guidance. One woman was advised to take a holiday. Any discussion was usually with the woman alone and rarely with both partners. In two cases the social worker suggested a separation order or divorce, but in seven others where the woman talked about leaving she was dissuaded from doing so. One file recorded 'She was thinking of leaving her husband again. Pointed out she had Christopher (son) to consider in this and her husband's feelings for the baby and herself. Reminded her that she had married and had to accept the consequences' (p. 130).

This study suggested that 'whatever the nature of the presenting problem', social workers were primarily concerned with women in their role as wives and mothers and tended to treat them 'as appendages of their families rather than as individuals in their own right' (p. 133). Ironically, the mere suspicion of child abuse results in swift intervention that takes precedence over concern for family unity and domestic privacy, whereas certain knowledge of wife abuse is often handled very differently. Borkowski and colleagues (1983) commented on the frequency with which social workers used value-laden terms such as 'immature' and 'unstable', as though there were agreed norms of behaviour appropriate to certain age groups. These researchers concluded that social workers looked, often quite cursorily, for evidence in the client's circumstances and history that fitted their favoured theories, without making careful assessments to check whether the facts of the situation supported their assumptions. The Dobashes (1985) have shown that the pattern of domestic violence is quite diverse and the way it occurs is likely to change over time. A direct and positive approach to both partners at an early stage is particularly important, as men like Roy in the first case example may feel deep remorse and be able to bring their violent feelings and frustration under sufficient control. Others may have 'a fantastic facility for saying they are sorry – and so it goes on until the next time' (Borkowski *et al.*, 1983, p. 121). The motivation for change is more easily explored in discussion with both partners together, but offering an appointment to the man via his wife is often counter-productive and may suggest that the social worker is not particularly anxious to see him. Borkowski and colleagues (1983) found that some social workers readily accepted that 'often the men don't want to talk anyway. Either it's an infringement of his privacy, a slight to his self-respect, or he just isn't used to talking about problems like this' (p. 150).

Local authorities may be loath to rehouse battered women and their children (Binney, Harkell and Nixon, 1985) and the police may also be unhelpful. A report (unpublished) commissioned recently by the Metropolitan Police urges the police to prosecute men for domestic violence even when the victim withdraws her complaint. The report points to experience in Canada where a complaint of domestic violence leads to a specially trained male-female police team visiting the home with a family consultant. The consultant may stay behind after the police leave, to support the woman or the family and to continue discussions. Prosecutions are likely to proceed even where the woman withdraws her allegations. This use of crisis intervention techniques, backed by the authority of the police and the courts, offers a model that could be usefully followed in this country.

From crisis theory to systems theory

As Palazzoli (1984) says, the most useful moment to begin to understand in what way a family is functioning is precisely the moment at which one of its members calls for help. 'Human games are by nature strategic, they proceed through moves and counter moves made by the different participants in the game . . . To appeal to an expert is one kind of family move, and . . . the very fact of calling us is the most recent move in the . . . game' (p. 306). Game-playing metaphors help us focus on interactions rather than on individual reactions: they are not meant to trivialise human pain and suffering, nor to underestimate the problems of weighing individual needs against family needs.

Crisis intervention may be more effective if, instead of working on a one-to-one basis with individuals, workers see themselves as 'intervening in a social system – as part of a network of relationships – and not as a single resource' (Rapoport, 1965, p. 30). Langsley and colleagues (1968) give similar advice, recommending that 'those who investigate crisis should look at the family setting in which they arise' (p. 155). It is also important to consider wider contextual issues such as racial and cultural influences and the worker's own values. Social workers who are strongly committed to particular principles, such as the need to free women from male oppression, have an ideological mooring-post which may prevent them feeling all at sea in chaotic and threatening situations. However, assessments based on a single, limited standpoint may be inadequate: we must guard against personal biases or ideologies which may lead us unconsciously into a coalition with a particular sub-system of a family or organisational system (Palazzoli, 1984). Very difficult questions arise in trying to balance the conflicting and sometimes irreconcilable interests of men and women, children and parents, private life and public values. None of us can offer a perfect balance to rectify gross imbalances of need or power and in moving swiftly to contain destructive crises we need to assess and re-assess our own role and objectives.

3

Helping Children Cope with Separation and Divorce

Divorce . . . is getting to be more accepted because society is growing and changing and divorce isn't a dirty word anymore . . . it's upsetting, but just because your parents are separated it doesn't mean you're going to lose anybody
(Zach, aged 13).

I think when parents get divorced, they both have special responsibility towards their children . . . The most important thing for parents to do is to help their children to understand why they got a divorce. They should let them think about the divorce as much as they want and let them ask as many questions as they feel like.
(Lulu, aged 8).

I was nine when my parents separated and it was a total shock to me . . . it really affected me emotionally. I just felt bad all the time.
(Meredith, aged 14).

When I think back over the past eight years, it seems as if I was just in one court and out the other, and half the time I didn't know what was going on. I went to about four different psychiatrists, but they didn't help, and the kids at school teased me when they found out I was going.
(Jimmy, aged 10).

47

The hardest thing for me about visiting my father is when I have to leave, and that makes me feel bad – and mad – inside. I still wish I could see him every day like I did when I was little.

(Caleb, aged 7).

Adults often find it very hard to help children cope with the pain of separation and divorce. Parents may avoid discussing their decisions with their children because they are so upset and confused themselves. They may also believe they are protecting their children by not telling them what is going on, in case it upsets them. Social workers and other professionals may discuss the problems of divorce only with the parents, perhaps because they lack experience in working with children and fear increasing their distress. But we underestimate children's perceptiveness and the isolation they experience if we talk *about* them instead of *with* them, without giving them the information and reassurance they need about decisions that directly concern them. The sensitive and thought-provoking book (Krementz, 1985) from which the quotations at the beginning of this chapter are taken (pp. 10–11, 17, 23, 25, 33, 72) may jolt us into recognising that even young children can have more understanding of the emotional consequences of separation than adults may imagine. But how do we consult children without giving them inappropriate influence and responsibility, and how do we select priorities in working with families split by separation or divorce? Should we concentrate on helping the children, or try to help their parents deal with pressing financial and housing problems? A parent who is distraught with worry about paying the rent and other bills may be too exhausted to respond to the children's anxiety and distress. Social workers need to be sensitive to the great pressures on parents, offering them as much encouragement and support as possible, since any suggestion that they are 'not good enough' as parents might result in their giving up completely.

Children's reactions to parental separation

Recent research studies both in Britain and the United States (Wallerstein and Kelly, 1980; Walczak and Burns, 1984;

Mitchell, 1985) suggest that whereas adults argue about the rights and wrongs of divorce, children generally agree, despite social class differences. Almost all children want their parents to stay together, and if this is impossible, they usually want to know that neither parent has abandoned them nor has any intention of doing so. Children themselves stress that they need information and explanations about changes in living arrangements, the right to be listened to as well as talked to and the right not to carry responsibility for painful decisions. The research studies referred to above suggest that the ways in which separated parents handle emotional conflict and the restructuring of family relationships may be even more important for their children's psychological health and educational attainment than poverty and poor housing conditions. This may present a dilemma for social workers and others who feel that if they direct their energies towards helping individual families, they are simply propping up fundamentally unsound economic and social policies. But if we choose to be active at a broader political level, we should be careful, as Haley (1976 p. 5) says, not to let the need for changes in public policy distract us from difficult, stressful work with troubled parents and their children.

Most of the early studies of the consequences of divorce for children took broad groups of children from 'intact' and 'broken' homes and looked for statistical differences between the two groups. Not surprisingly, the results of these studies were not conclusive, since there is probably as much variation within these groups as between them. Comparisons may be misleading for a number of reasons: separation may take place some time before the divorce and children usually react more acutely to the separation than to the divorce itself. Moreover, separation can occur in many different ways, either in a sudden crisis or as part of a long drawn-out and recurring process, so the point at which children's reactions are measured needs to be related to the time-scale of the separation and divorce. A permanent separation between parents can take place at different stages in children's physical and emotional development and these developmental differences combined with differences of temperament make it unlikely that siblings will be affected by parental separation in the same way. Rutter (1971) concluded from his review of the literature on parent-child separation that it is the ongoing disturbance in family relationships which does the damage, rather than the separation *per se*. Hetherington, Cox and Cox (1982) also found in their empirical research that children's emotional and behavioural problems were usually associated with current parental conflict, rather than with previous marital conflict.

Adults and children – a clash of interests?

In the past, unhappily married couples were expected to stay together for the sake of the children, whereas many people now believe that it is better for children if their parents separate, rather than subjecting them to perpetual conflict in the home. Wallerstein and Kelly (1980) found however in their well-known study of divorcing families in California that although divorce benefited many of the adults, the children did not experience comparable benefits. A significant number of children suffered serious damage to their psychological health, not only in the short term but in adolescence as well. For most of the children, the changes brought by separation and divorce were no less stressful than the previous marital conflict. These families may have contained a disproportionate number of families who were experiencing particularly severe problems and it would be unsafe to base generalised conclusions on this self-selected group. However, Mitchell's (1985) Scottish study based on a representative sample of families reinforces Wallerstein and Kelly's findings. With few exceptions, the children in both studies wanted their parents to stay together, despite severe problems in the home. Even when there was acute disharmony and constant rows, very few children reacted to their parents' separation with relief or saw it as a solution to the family's problems. Later on, as they grew up, some of them came to realise that the divorce had been a necessary and even constructive step for one or both parents, but this understanding was not usually available to the children when they most needed it. Wallerstein and Kelly found that few children could identify with either parent's wish to escape from an unhappy marriage and most of them found the separation and its aftermath acutely stressful. In addition to the shock of one parent's often unexplained disappearance, they suffered from the diminished care and attention of the parent who remained, since this parent was often too preoccupied to give the children the reassurance and support they desperately needed. Over half the children in these families felt that their lives had been totally disrupted and fewer than ten per cent expressed relief despite, in some cases, having witnessed physical violence between their parents. Wallerstein and Kelly expected when they embarked on their study that the children would experience a sense of relief in direct proportion to the level of conflict between their parents. Yet no such finding emerged. Younger children experienced relief only when they themselves felt afraid of their father's violence and older children also opposed the separation unless they understood it as a remedy for insoluble problems. The level and duration of the distress experienced by many of the children in this study are poignantly conveyed by the researchers and few studies can have done more to alert adults to the depth of misery and loneliness which a child is liable to experience when a loved parent leaves home. Wallerstein and Kelly found that a quarter of the children and adolescents in their study were seriously troubled and depressed a year after the divorce. About one-sixth seemed completely taken up with their intense yearning for the absent parent and/or for a more satisfying and secure relationship with the remaining parent. Some of these children, particularly the younger ones, showed a marked regression in their development and functioning, whereas others seemed to suffer only a temporary setback. Richards and Dyson (1982) concluded from their review of research on the effects of parental separation and divorce on children that there are many complex variables affecting children's adjustment in the short and longer term. They noticed that what seemed to help children most was sometimes contrary both to popular opinion and to professional advice and practice. For example, the amount of time children spend with the other parent seems to matter more to them than how often they see this parent, whereas adults usually concentrate on the frequency of access visits rather than on their length.

Walczak and Burns (1984) interviewed a hundred children, young people and adults, ranging in age from six to fifty-seven, who volunteered to talk about their experience of parental divorce. 17 per cent said it had brought some relief, but 26 per cent felt the divorce had affected them very badly and 32 per cent said the consequences had been very mixed. When they were asked to identify what had been the worst feature for them as children, 'feeling upset about poor communication' headed the list by a long way. Mitchell (1985) found similarly that while just over a third of the parents in her sample had apparently given some explanation to their children, nearly two-thirds had not explained any-thing, often because they thought the reasons for the separ-ation were 'obvious'. Several mothers said they had been too ill with their 'nerves' to be able to talk with their children and one mother explained: 'I didn't even take it in myself for five months. I was too shocked' (p. 58). Mitchell compared accounts given by parents and children in the same family and found that mothers' descriptions of their children's reactions differed from the children's self-reports almost as often as they tallied. One mother admitted she had been too upset to notice her son's feelings and a girl who had been taken to her grandmother's house at the age of ten said 'My Mum didn't understand how I felt. She was too busy being angry' (p. 94).

Children may find it very difficult to ask one parent when they can see the other one, especially if they are aware that this question may cause further pain and anger. They may be very attentive and protective towards a vulnerable parent and their strong sense of loyalty towards both parents can increase their isolation. Children's efforts to hide their feelings may combine with their parents' inability to explain, building a wall of silence around the parent who has left home. The longer this wall remains, the harder it generally becomes to dismantle it.

Interpreting children's reactions

Parents who disagree about custody and access arrangements tend to interpret their children's feelings and behaviour in ways which support their own preferences or point of view. It is quite possible that neither parent understands the child's painfully tangled feelings and the following examples of typical arguments between parents show the conflicting conclusions they may lead to. It is adapted from a report by Justice (1975), the British section of the International Commission of Jurists.

1. Children's reluctance or refusal to go on access visits is explained:
   (a) by the caretaking parent as the result of the child's fear, anger, dislike or indifference towards the visiting parent; or to similar feelings towards the other parent's new partner and/or other children who are present; or to the visiting parent's irregular visits, unpunctuality, failure to look after the children properly and attempts to use them as allies, spies, messengers, etc.
   (b) by the absent parent as the result of indoctrination by the caretaking parent, who uses every opportunity to turn the children against the parent they no longer live with; or that the children are afraid of being punished or rejected by the parent they live with if they show affection and loyalty towards the absent parent.

2. Children's eagerness to go on access visits is ascribed by:
   (a) the caretaking parent to bribery and spoiling by the visiting parent, to lack of discipline on access visits, and the fact that the visiting parent provides his or her undivided attention for a short space of time, free from household chores and often with more money to spend.
   (b) by the visiting parent to the children's strong attachment and/or relief at getting away from a depressed/bitter/neglectful caretaking parent.

3. Staying access may be considered:
   (a) undesirable by the caretaking parent on many different grounds. The other parent (usually, the father) may not have experience in feeding and looking after the children and may be seen as an incompetent or unreliable parent. If he or she is living with someone else, this other person may be seen as a bad influence who is likely to contaminate the

children. A child who is being treated for emotional or health problems may be thought to need special handling which the visiting parent cannot be trusted to provide.

(b) highly desirable by the visiting parent, so that the children can spend enough time to sustain or build a close relationship. This parent needs to do ordinary, normal things with the children such as giving them meals and putting them to bed, whereas short outings in public places are often artificial and lacking in intimacy. Longer visits including overnight stays give space not only for positive relationships to develop but also for conflicts in which children test out the reliability of the visiting parent's control and care.

4. Children's tears, rudeness, bad behaviour, sleep disturbances, illness etc. after visits are explained:

(a) by the caretaking parent as evidence of their unhappiness during the visit; or by the poor care or bad influence of the visiting parent or other people involved; by the disruptive effects of moving from one parent to the other; and as signs that the children need more time and security in their own home/with their own friends; and so on.

(b) by the visiting parent as evidence of the children's unhappiness at home with the caretaking parent; or by the poor care or bad influence of that parent or other people in the household; or by the children's need to spend more time with the visiting parent; and so on.

5. The remedy for these problems is to:

(a) reduce access visits or stop them altogether.

(b) increase access visits, or apply for custody, care and control.

This clash of perceptions and conclusions may be handled by parents in much the same way as they handled the problems in their marriage. Arguments may be uncontrolled and destructive, with angry scenes conducted in front of the children in a conscious or unconscious bid for their support. Couples who avoid direct confrontation may carry on the fight by proxy: solicitors and other professionals may be enlisted on one side or the other and a private argument between parents may escalate into a full-scale legal battle. Some couples wage war on each other on all fronts – face to face, as well as via solicitors, relatives and the children. Alternatively, one parent may feel the odds are so heavily loaded in the other's favour that the only possible course is to withdraw altogether. These fight-or-flight reactions obviously affect the children and they may learn to deal with conflict in the same negative ways.

Family dynamics and children's adjustment

Very few research studies so far have taken an interactional approach in exploring how the various ways in which separated parents resolve, continue or escape from marital conflict affect their children's subsequent adjustment and development, both at home and at school. Lund and Riley's research (Lund, 1984) is therefore particularly important because children's emotional adjustment and educational progress were studied in the context of family relationships and dynamics. Socio-economic factors, including parents' income and education, were taken into account and the findings were compared with a small control group of 'intact' families. The researchers explored children's feelings about their families and themselves by means of game-playing techniques, such as the Bene Anthony Family Relations test, and found that the families fell into three main groups, which they described as 'harmonious co-parent families', 'conflicted co-parent families' and 'absent parent families'. The 'harmonious co-parent families' were not devoid of conflict but these parents made a conscious effort to co-operate, generally managing to work out access arrangements without going to court and sometimes attending school functions together. Most of the fathers played an active part in their children's lives and regular staying access every other weekend was a common pattern. Both the parents and the teachers in this group commented very positively on the children's adjustment and attitudes. The children were rated as having good self-esteem and the amount of emotional disturbance as recorded by their teachers was lower than average for this age group as a whole.

About a third of the families in Lund and Riley's study were termed 'conflicted co-parent families' because the parents continued to battle with each other long after their divorce. These couples were likely to have returned to court several times with disputes over access and there was usually conflict over financial matters as well. The fathers persisted in their attempts to see the children while the mothers struggled to obtain regular maintenance. Their battles were usually conducted via solicitors but the parents' anger and frustration sometimes erupted in physical violence and one father was arrested for assault. Their children expressed more anger than the other children, criticising their parents for failing to sort things out but at least seeing the problems as their parents' responsibility. These children were less well adjusted at school than the children of 'harmonious co-parents' but better adjusted than the children in the 'absent parent' group, described below.

The third group in Lund and Riley's study represents the substantial proportion of divorced families in which contact is lost between the children and one parent. In these families, access visits never became established and sooner or later they stopped altogether. The men were more likely to have been physically violent to their wives, who were usually anxious to be free of them though some mothers tried to persuade the father to visit his children. One mother said 'It hurts, I suppose, because he will not commit himself to visiting on a regular basis, which I felt was absolutely essential.' Paradoxically, the fathers were usually portrayed as caring about their children before the separation and seemingly could not bear the pain of seeing the children for a short time and then parting from them again. One man who was interviewed said that he was angry to be told by social workers and the courts how to be a father to his own children. He said he would either be a father on his own terms, which as far as he was concerned meant resuming the marriage, or he would not be a father at all. The children in this group were rated by their teachers as having the highest number of emotional problems and the lowest self-esteem, compared with the other groups. Despite the lack of contact, fathers remained important to their children but instead of blaming either parent for the break-up these children tended to blame themselves. Depression and low self-esteem were associated with under-achievement at school and the researchers concluded that children are liable to suffer even more from the loss of a parent than from continuing parental conflict. However, as these depressed children tend to withdraw into a shell of silent distress, parents and professionals are less likely to realise that they need help.

A close relationship with the remaining parent mitigates the loss of the other parent, but Wallerstein and Kelly (1977) found that if it is very close, children may find it hard to break free and live their own lives. Many of the young people they talked with felt they had been given premature responsibility to support a sick or distressed parent or look after younger siblings. Although this gave them a sense of achievement, many felt their childhood and adolescence had been significantly burdened by taking on a quasi-parental role.

These research studies provide strong reasons for maintaining children's access to the parent who leaves home, despite the difficulties that are often involved. Briefly, these reasons may be summarised as follows:

1. Children need to know that they are not responsible for the separation and that they have not lost the absent parent's love. This knowledge helps maintain their trust in the reliability of relationships and safeguards their capacity to form lasting attachments themselves in adult life. If children feel rejected, they may react by rejecting the parent who has hurt them. This rejection may be encouraged overtly or covertly by the remaining parent and children may learn to use rejection as a means of dealing with personal conflict.

2. Children need information about their origins as a means of establishing their own identity and avoiding fantasies that an absent parent (whom they may physically resemble) is 'bad', or too busy and important to care about them (Benians, 1986). They may become very anxious about a parent who is said to be ill or in prison, and as they mature they need to understand why their parents were

unable to live together. If they are helped to understand why and how relationships break down, children are better prepared for the problems they may meet as adults, but these opportunities for learning are often missed. A 22-year-old girl quoted by Wallerstein (1982, p. 12) said: 'I felt pretty happy after the divorce. At least my mom and dad weren't going to fight any more. The divorce changed my life for the better because I got away from my dad.' She then went on to relate that she had married at eighteen and divorced her first husband at the age of twenty-one.

3. Loss of contact between a child and one parent often severs contact with other relatives as well. Grandparents may be very important figures in a child's life and the sudden loss of one set of grandparents, uncles, aunts and cousins can cause much additional grief, as well as putting a heavy burden on the remaining parent to compensate for the loss of a network of caring relatives. Many single parents have great difficulty in coping, at least in the first stages of adjusting to separation, and all available sources of support should be preserved wherever possible.

4. There is evidence (Wallerstein and Kelly, 1980; Richards and Dyson, 1982) that allowing children to maintain good relationships with both natural parents helps rather than hinders them in forming new relationships with step-parents. This is often not appreciated by remarried parents who tend to see former partners as a threat to the stability of the new family. From the child's point of view, parents are not usually disposable and interchangable and a step-parent may be deeply resented if he or she is foisted on them as a substitute for a parent who is greatly missed.

Children's roles in family conflict

Adults often assume that children are passive victims of family breakup and they may indeed be onlookers who sadly watch their familiar world disintegrate into fragments of unexplained events. However, as Montalvo and Haley (1973) and other family therapists have pointed out, a child's behaviour is not only an individual response: it may be an attempt to influence other members of the family and deal with an overwhelming crisis for the family as whole. To say this is not to blame children in any way nor to suggest that the trouble between their parents is their fault. Their largely unconscious survival strategies may be a desperate attempt to obtain the love and security they need, to preserve the family as they know it and to give their parents the love and support of which they too may be in dire need.

Early theories of emotional disturbance in children assumed a linear cause-effect relationship between dysfunctional marital relationships and their impact on children. More recently, however, family therapists have helped us understand that family interactions follow a circular rather than linear pattern (see for example Bentovim, Gorell Barnes and Cooklin, 1982). These repetitive, revolving patterns can be seen very clearly in access problems during and after divorce. Saposnek (1983, p. 120) suggests that children become 'innocent but functional contributors' in family problems and therefore need to be actively involved in their resolution. A child's behaviour which may seem totally negative and counter-productive when viewed from an individual perspective may become comprehensible as a coping strategy, when viewed from a family systems perspective.

Reuniting strategies

Stress-related physical symptoms and troublesome behaviour may reflect children's conscious or unconscious attempts to bring their parents together again, even if they themselves suffer more pain or punishment in the process. A sick child may deflect parents' attention from their marital problems and unite them in concern for the child, but this strategy requires the child to remain ill, since the marital conflict is liable to re-surface once the child recovers. It may also rebound on the child in other ways, by giving one parent a weapon to use against the other. Complaints of headaches and stomach aches may be interpreted as a sign that access visits are harming the child and the custodial parent may ask a doctor or social worker to recommend that access should be stopped. Occasionally children seem to want this outcome themselves, rarely because they want to lose touch permanently with the parent who has left but because they sense that the custodial parent badly needs their protection and support. Wallerstein and Kelly (1980) found that pre-latency children aged six to nine were particularly likely to form a protective alliance with the parent whom they perceived as most hurt and vulnerable. They were liable to sacrifice their own needs in order to help this parent as best they could.

Sometimes a child offers himself unconsciously (and sometimes consciously) as a scapegoat who draws the parents' anger on himself as a way of deflecting the hostility between them. Saposnek (1983) describes how children's delinquency, non-school attendance or aggressive behaviour may provoke rows between parents, keeping them emotionally involved with the child and with each other. The continuation of these problems may be necessary for the family because they prevent one parent withdrawing altogether. It is important therefore not to assume that parents or children want to end the problems or symptoms they complain of. Distressing or disruptive behaviour may have a positive function in maintaining relationships in families, and one or more members will probably hold on to this behaviour until deeper needs are attended to.

Case example – running to the other parent

Gary, aged 12, was repeatedly absent from school with complaints of stomach ache. He was unhappy at the move from a small junior school to a large comprehensive and on several occasions he cycled to his father's flat when his mother thought he had gone to school. His father had left home some months previously to live with a divorced woman who had three children of her own. As he worked shifts, he was often home in the mornings and let Gary come in for a while, but then became worried that he was seriously unhappy and unwell. On the third occasion he telephoned his wife to tell her Gary was with him. Her reaction was to drive straight over to the flat, drag the sobbing Gary into her car and deposit him angrily at school. The father then saw a solicitor to discuss whether he should seek custody of Gary and the mother went to her solicitor to ask if Gary could be stopped from seeing his father because he was discouraging him from going to school. A full-scale legal battle was then brewing, ignoring Gary's signal that he needed love and support from both parents, their co-operation in helping him settle down in the new school and reassurance that although they had separated, neither of them was abandoning him.

Engaging parents and children simultaneously

Gary's behaviour was not only an expression of his own anxiety and depression. It may also have been a response to the emotional need he sensed in both his parents to remain involved with each other. Gary was partly acting as his mother's messenger in seeking attention from his father and he may well have picked up some ambivalence in his father too. There was evident need to help his parents, but working only with them might not have helped Gary sufficiently with his own feelings of loneliness, confusion and fear for the future.

It is not easy, however, to address different generations simultaneously and to gain the trust of parents and children at the same time. Focusing on Gary's needs and interpreting them to his parents might have increased their feelings of guilt and inadequacy, resulting in one or both refusing further appointments. Working with Gary on his own would have brought the worker face to face with his pain, without necessarily being able to give him the reassurance he was looking for. There are great dilemmas for social workers in focusing on parental needs and problems or, alternatively, taking on the role of child advocate or child therapist. If the worker becomes too closely identified with the child, this may increase parents' anxiety or resistance and it may be difficult to tell parents what the child has said, as this can cause trouble for the child. Encouraging children to talk privately and promising them confidentiality is risky because information might have to be acted on in order to protect the child. The Court of Appeal has instructed judges that they must not promise confidentiality to children if they interview them privately, as this might result in injustice to one parent and/or the children themselves. (This instruction was given in the case of Elder and Elder, *Family Law*, 1986, vol. 16, p. 190. Social workers need to be equally careful not to promise total confidentiality to children, nor to base their decisions solely on statements made by children under stress. As Kell (1986, p. 17) points out, direct questioning by adults may elicit only replies which the child thinks the adult needs or wants to hear, assuming that the questions were understood in the first place.

The wishes of the child

The DHSS Code of Practice on Access to Children in Care (1983) states that local authorities must 'give due consideration to the child's wishes and feelings, having regard to his age and understanding' (para. 11). The House of Commons Social Services Committee on Children in Care (1984) also emphasised that social workers should seek 'an explicit statement of a child's wishes' from the child, and that older children should attend reviews at which decisions are to be taken concerning their future (par. 243). Some children, especially older ones, can express their views very clearly and welcome the chance to do so. But younger and/or anxious ones may deal with their divided loyalties by aligning themselves at different times with each parent and saying what they feel each parent needs to hear. A welfare officer or social worker may then be expected to interview the child to find out 'the truth'. Each facet of this complex, multi-faceted 'truth' may however be equally true, at least subjectively, and it may be very difficult to understand children's divided and half-expressed feelings, especially if they are seen only once or twice during a family crisis. The more the child has become triangulated in conflict between the parents, the more pressure there will be on the child to respond to conflicting messages from each parent.

Court counsellors in the Family Court of Australia (Marshall, Grant and Nasser, 1979) argue that the concept of 'the wishes of the child' is simplistic, misleading and even damaging to the child. They suggest it is more appropriate to think in terms of 'the needs, perceptions and attachments of the child', recognising that a whole range of factors needs to be taken into account in establishing what a child may be responding to in expressing a particular view or in avoiding doing so. These factors include children's age and stage of development, their temperament and verbal skills, the previous and current family situation and the child's perceptions of each parent's actions and feelings. Social workers also need to understand that family or cultural traditions may prevent children voicing their own feelings. For example, Asian children may steadfastly refuse to answer questions about their family as they may have been taught to remain silent on such matters.

The Principal Divorce Registry in London asks parents to bring children of nine and over to in-court conciliation appointments, where the children are the subject of custody or access disputes. The court has no special facilities for children and what they say in these brief interviews with a welfare officer may effectively decide the outcome of the case. Davis (1982b) observed conciliation appointments at Bristol County Court in which children were involved. He expressed concern that when children had apparently said they did not want to see one parent, an order for no access might be made although this might be at considerable emotional cost to the child, at the time or subsequently.

Communicating with children

If children are to feel sufficiently secure to be able to share their feelings with adults they scarcely know, it is important to provide them with a friendly environment, well-stocked with play equipment to help them show feelings they may be unable to put into words. As Haley (1976, p. 29) says, toys and play activities allow action in the room rather than merely conversation about action. There may be reasons for seeing children on their own, but seeing them with their parents is often a better way of helping parents and children communicate with each other. In the case of Joanne, a 15-year-old caught in a custody dispute between her parents, it was helpful to give her an opportunity to talk on her own about her school, friendships and plans for the future. Her parents appreciated this need and after Joanne had talked with the social worker, a family discussion took place in which Joanne and her parents talked more freely than before. In another case, both parents recognised that their sons, aged seven and eleven, needed some explanations and reassurance concerning their father that neither parent could give them directly at that particular stage. It was therefore agreed that the worker would see the boys to give them positive messages which they needed to hear, rather than seeking information from them. This meeting was one stage in a sequence of work with the parents and the children.

Winnicott (1977) emphasises the importance of social workers communicating directly *with* children and not simply working *for* them. 'The actual presence of the social worker reduces isolation and loneliness, and communicates concern and support. In times of acute distress the actual physical holding of a child is likely to be the only means of bringing relief' (p. 8). The social worker may be the only person apart from the child who is in direct contact with both halves of the split family. Children may be relieved to discover that someone else is sharing this stressful role of go-between and knows how it feels.

Some welfare officers (Howard and Shepherd, 1982; Guise, 1983) believe that parents and children should always be seen together from the outset, particularly where children have become triangulated into parental conflict. Family meetings are however often difficult to arrange in practice, and the prospect of violent arguments in the children's presence may arouse anxieties for the worker as well as for the family. Carpenter and Treacher (1983) observed in relation to family therapy that children may be withdrawn and uncommunicative, stubbornly refusing to take any part. Or they can be noisy and disruptive, making professionals feel embarrassed and ineffective and thus losing their credibility in the parents' eyes. Workers who feel uncertain how to involve children may resort to counselling the parents, talking over the children's heads as though they were not there at all. On the other hand, those who are skilled at engaging sympathetically with children and gaining their confidence may find they have set up barriers between themselves and the parents, by making the parents feel inadequate. Counsellors working in a pioneer divorce counselling agency in West Germany (Parkinson, 1986b) tended at first to go along with parents' objections to the children being present. However, as they gained experience they found it essential to involve the children. They found this helped parents focus on their children as individuals, instead of using them as bargaining counters. Children of any age can listen and take part in some way, without being compelled to speak. The Munich counsellors find that most of the children they see with their parents are under six, while the second largest group involves children aged six to twelve. Many children show their joy at seeing the absent parent, thus making it impossible for the caretaking parent to oppose access on the grounds that these visits upset the children. But there are other confused and sad children who cry and become very disturbed when their parents come in contact. The worker may then be confronted by two angry parents and mute children who are unable to confirm or contradict their parents' accounts of their feelings.

Children who refuse access visits

Social workers and the courts are often in a considerable quandary when a child steadfastly refuses to see the absent parent, despite assurances in some cases from the custodial parent that he or she has no objection to access taking place, 'if this is what the child wants'. Forcing a reluctant child to go out with a parent whom the child fears or hates may produce acute trauma for the child – and often both parents as well – and this stress may lead to behaviour problems and/or physical illness (James and Wilson, 1984). Wallerstein and Kelly (1980) found that almost a third of the children in their study felt intensely angry with one or both parents for breaking up the family and some of them, especially 9-to-12-year-old children, seemed angrier a year and a half after the separation than they had been initially. Their tendency to reject the parent whom they blamed for causing the break-up resulted in access taking place very little, if at all. However, if the refusal of access is accepted at face-value, children may feel even more wounded at being abandoned so easily, though their grief is often masked by apparent indifference or hostility. Wallerstein and Kelly concluded that pre-adolescent children were not reliable judges of their own best interests as they were liable to make erratic and sometimes self-sacrificing choices. Some children are so keenly aware of one parent's loneliness and fragility that they take on responsibilities far beyond their age, acting as a substitute spouse or parent in a reversal of roles which may be psychologically damaging to the child. By responding to the overwhelming emotional demands of a bereft parent, children may stifle their own need to see the other parent, sometimes rejecting a parent who is actually the more nurturing one.

Social workers have a very difficult task in understanding the particular dynamics which produce protective reactions from children. Even if they understand them, it may still be very difficult to work out whether and how to seek change. Some parents may be helped by discussing their children's reactions and how to help them cope with their divided loyalties. In one such case, the mother realised that she needed to reassure her 4-year-old daughter, Becky, that she (the mother) would enjoy visiting a friend of hers while Becky was out with her father and that she would be safely back again by the time he brought Becky home. This gave Becky emotional permission to go out with her father and reduced her fear that her mother might be missing when she came home. Parents with good verbal skills may be able to grasp and apply new ideas relatively easily, but many social work clients are seriously lacking in verbal skills and those from ethnic minority groups may have major language problems. Social workers need skills in non-verbal as well as verbal methods of communicating with families, so that they can help parents and children express feelings they may be unable to put into words. Some of them lack the words they need, and many are afraid to use the words they do possess.

The use of play materials

O'Brien and Loudon (1985) point out that there are two languages in common usage, the language of visual images as well as the spoken word. They urge those who work with families to avoid the exclusive use of only one of these languages and to collect a range of inexpensive materials that can be used imaginatively with children of different ages and their families. These can include 'stick and peel houses' (Uniset) and Wedgie Play People (Galt Toys), finger and glove puppets, paper and drawing materials, jigsaws with figures that fit into a wooden frame, mobiles and weighing scales that can be used to illustrate emotional imbalances in families. Wooden rods of varying lengths can be used to illustrate a child's need for firm links and reliable boundaries, as well as showing who is in contact with whom. In the case of Gary who was mentioned earlier, the Wedgie figures would have been too childish but the rods could have been used to look at each family member's sources of support. Both Gary and his mother felt lonely and unsupported and it may be possible to normalise disturbing feelings by emphasising how common they are, as well as considering where more support could come from.

Separated fathers often have no clear role in the divided family and jigsaws or other toys may help children and parents look at who fits where, in relation to the child's daily life at home and at school. Some fathers do not know the names of the child's best friends or teacher and may not have thought to ask. Their apparent lack of interest may feel like rejection to the child and some parents need encouragement just to talk naturally about everyday things. Jason, aged nine, said: 'I took my project to show Dad but he didn't look at it'. The worker said: 'Maybe your Dad didn't understand that you wanted him to look at it' and Jason and his father then talked about the things they could do together next time. This helped Jason's mother as well, as she complained about her husband's lack of interest in the children. Appendix A lists some books that may be helpful to children and their parents.

A parent who feels very hurt and angry may feel however that the parent who has left home has no right to be involved with the children any more. This parent may not only deny access but refuse to pass on any information about the child, as a way of maintaining sole control and sometimes as a means of punishing the other parent. If parents and young children are encouraged to look at pictures or other images relating to the child's daily life and activities, this may help parents realise that they have different things to contribute, without needing to compete as rivals for the child's affections. Even if parents have different standards and ideas about how children should be brought up, this need not be an insuperable obstacle unless injury or neglect is alleged. Sooner or later, children have to work out their own standards and once they go to school they can see that there are alternative models to choose from. Parents who constantly denigrate each other, either directly to the child or in the child's hearing, may not realise the effect this has on children. Some workers use sculpting or other techniques to help families gain insight into the non-verbal messages they give each other.

Play materials need to be selected carefully to engage parents and children in discussion and joint problem-solving (Ross, 1985). Children of all ages can be included and even toddlers who seem absorbed in playing on the floor are likely to absorb a great deal of what is said and particularly the tone and manner in which it is said. Sometimes it is helpful to rehearse with a family exactly how an access visit will be managed, using finger-puppets or play-figures to act out the to-ing and fro-ing that will take place. This may reduce some of the anxieties about separation that children and parents often feel. Fresh possibilities may emerge which none of the family has thought of before, such as sometimes allowing one child to have one parent to themselves for a whole day or afternoon instead of assuming that all the children must always go on access visits together. Court orders for access rarely provide for this degree of flexibility. Some movement may be achieved in stuck situations if arrangements are considered for each of the children individually, instead of treating them as a 'package deal'.

There are now special access centres in some areas where parents can leave and collect their children on neutral ground, without having to meet each other. Volunteer helpers are usually at hand to welcome parents and children and generally to ease the hand-over, if help is needed. Most of these centres use existing facilities and the waiting-areas usually have refreshments and toys to occupy children while they wait for a parent to collect them.

Groupwork with children

There cannot be any rigid prescriptions for working with children because each child and each family situation is unique. Social workers need to have a range of working methods that they can match to particular situations. Some very disturbed children need longer-term supportive help which may involve play therapy alone with the child over a period of time (Jewett, 1984). Until the late seventies, post-divorce therapy with the whole family was rarely contemplated, but as Goldman and Coane (1977) pointed out, this can provide a critical opportunity to redefine family relationships and clarify generational boundaries. They assert that what seemed too hot to handle ten years ago is too hot *not* to handle today. However, prolonged family therapy after divorce may suggest to the children that their parents are getting back together again, making it harder for the children and parents to accept that the marriage is actually over.

Wallerstein and Kelly recognise in another of their joint articles (Kelly and Wallerstein, 1977) that although some children need extended specialist treatment for severe disturbance, the huge numbers of children experiencing divorce make individual help in each case a practical impossibility. American and British experience of running groups for children whose families are affected by divorce or separation suggests that these groups can be very helpful. Children and parents can gain a lot of support and insight from each other. Kessler and Bostwick (1977) described their use of a whole-day Saturday workshop for children aged ten to sixteen, advertised through helping agencies and in the local press. First, there was a warming-up phase in which the children were asked to find a partner and introduce themselves to each other (for example, choosing two adjectives that they thought described themselves best). They then moved on to a series of structured tasks designed to facilitate sharing, acceptance and group support. The children were taught that it is possible to express negative feelings in a constructive way and they then practised these methods, role-playing different scenarios and discussing what was awkward or difficult. Kessler and Bostwick found that despite their initial anxiety, the children were responsive, perceptive and hard-working and in many ways they progressed more quickly and easily than adults usually do.

Parents can also be encouraged to bring their children to a divorce experience course, using the model pioneered in this country by Leicestershire Probation Service. (Leicestershire Divorce Court Welfare Service, 'Divorce Experience Course – A Guide for Staff Members', January 1979.) These courses usually run once a week for about three weeks. In the first session, adults are helped to look at different dimensions of the divorce process and are then encouraged to share some of their own experience in small discussion groups. Children are invited to the final session, when two or three different groups may cater for children of different ages, using games, discussion or role-play. Consumer reactions to these courses are usually extremely positive and although they take a good deal of preparation and involve extra evening work, there are benefits for the social workers who run them, such as closer links with other agencies and opportunities to learn from each other. This can mirror the learning that takes place for individual parents and children – that sharing feelings and difficulties with other people often makes the feelings more manageable and may solve particular problems.

4

Who Decides about the Children?

Mother: 'We need a judge with the wisdom of Solomon to decide about the children.'
Father: 'You know bloody well the mother always wins. I might as well give up.'

Parents' decisions in divorce

Parents who separate without divorcing can make their own decisions about their children unless one of them (or another party) applies to the magistrates' domestic court or to the High Court under wardship proceedings (Pearce, 1986). Informal separations are not recorded or controlled by the state and one hopes they never will be. But for reasons that may seem illogical today, the situation changes fundamentally once divorce or judicial separation is embarked on. The boundary of family privacy is then automatically breached wherever children under sixteen are involved, because English divorce law imposes a statutory responsibility on the courts to check whether 'the arrangements proposed for the children are satisfactory or the best that can be devised in the circumstances, or that it is impractical for the parents to make any such arrangements (Matrimonial Causes Act 1973, Section 41). In uncontested cases this check is carried out by a judge at the Section 41 or children's appointment, often in a brief and perfunctory interview lasting less than five minutes (Davis, MacLeod and Murch, 1983; Dodds, 1983). Some judges and welfare officers actively encourage both parents to

71

come to these appointments to discuss the arrangements for their children, referring them for conciliation or a welfare inquiry if there are difficulties. The courts are faced however with a very difficult balancing exercise in trying to maintain parents' autonomy while exercising their statutory duty to regard the welfare of the child as the first and paramount consideration. The result can be 'an unhappy compromise in which the parents think that the court settles the arrangements and the court thinks that the parents do' (Law Commission, 1986, p. 104). In this uncertainty between minimal interference in family life and the duty to consider the best interests of the child, neither the courts nor the parents themselves may actually identify and respond to the needs and feelings of children.

Northern Ireland follows a firmly interventionist policy in calling for a welfare report in all divorces involving children, usually from a social worker employed by one of the health and social services boards. However, research has shown (McCoy and Nelson, 1983) that nearly three-quarters of divorcing couples in Northern Ireland have been separated more than two years by the time the inquiry takes place. A social worker's appearance on the scene at this late stage may serve little purpose and there is now pressure to change the law so that a welfare inquiry is ordered only where there are known to be problems concerning the children. Scottish divorce courts already follow a policy of minimum intervention, referring only about 3 per cent of divorces to a children's reporter, who may be either a lawyer or a social worker. In the great majority of Scottish divorces, the court is given very scanty information about the children and may not even be told whether the child is seeing the non-custodial parent (Seale, 1984). No access order was made in 86 per cent of Scottish divorces in 1980 because the non-custodial parent made no application. If divorce proceedings are discontinued, the welfare inquiry is discontinued as well (In Scottish terminology it becomes labelled 'asleep') and the children's welfare receives no further attention from the court although there could at this stage be more cause for concern than when the inquiry was ordered.

American researchers (Kitson and Langlie, 1984) found

that couples who stopped their divorce proceedings halfway through often continued to lead very disruptive lives. Many of them remained in an emotional limbo, half married and half divorced, separating repeatedly and experiencing high levels of violence and distress. The children of these couples are liable to suffer more serious disturbance than those whose parents complete their divorce but they may not come to the attention of welfare authorities. Couples in this American study had seldom sought professional help, despite the seriousness of their problems.

The state's welfare net is therefore an arbitrary and unreliable filter where separating and divorcing families are concerned. Some children who badly need help may fall through large holes in the mesh, while many families who are managing relatively well are subjected to an unnecessary welfare check which they may resent.

Custody decisions

In 1985 over 100 000 custody orders were made in divorce and other family proceedings (Law Commission, 1986, para. 4.1). The term 'custody' is however both emotive and confusing in relation to children whose parents live apart. It suggests exclusive possession by one parent, rather than loving attention from both parents to the child's needs and interests. Some parents seize on the allocation of custody as another weapon which can be used in their continuing marital battle, though many of those who threaten to fight for custody do not ultimately pursue their fight through the courts. Only about 6 per cent of divorces involve a fully contested court hearing on custody but even this small proportion involves a large number of children – about 9000 children in 1985, which is almost twice the number of children annually committed to care in civil proceedings (Law Commission, 1986, para. 4.2). However, the absence of contested custody proceedings in the vast majority of divorces does not necessarily mean that the parents are in agreement. Eekelaar's observation (1984, p. 68) that 'in the vast majority of cases, parents agree their own arrangements' may be mistaken, since hostile acquiescence is not the same as real agreement. In a survey carried out by researchers at Bristol University (Davis, Macleod and Murch, 1982), parents who were not currently involved in contested custody or access proceedings reported high levels of disagreement which they had not referred to the court. As many as 29 per cent said they had disagreed over arrangements for the children and 18 per cent were still dissatisfied with the existing access arrangements. Some parents remain in a deadlock which neither of them seems motivated to resolve, while others turn to a more powerful source of authority – the court, the police or 'the welfare' – which they believe capable of restoring order in their lives and even of righting past wrongs. There are however powerful deterrents against taking a dispute to the court, such as the dread of court proceedings and the fear of ending up in a worse position than before. Some fathers see no point in going to court because they think courts always favour the mother. They may be advised by their solicitor not to apply for custody (Ambrose, Harper and Pemberton, 1983) and if they do not qualify for legal aid they may not feel confident to argue their own case in court against a legally qualified opponent.

The adversarial system is often blamed for increasing hostility between divorcing parents and legal labels such as 'sole custody' and 'non-custodial parent' may actually cause disputes between couples who otherwise agree about the care of their children (Patrician, 1984). Pearson and Thoennes (1984) found many custody disputes were about the idea that one parent (usually, the father) is disposable after divorce, not about which parent should have day-to-day care of the children. Divorcing parents often think 'custody' means 'care and control', but when it comes to practical arrangements, relatively few of them fight over the physical care of the children, as distinct from legal custody and/or access arrangements. In the small number of cases in which care and control is contested, possession tends to be nine-tenths of the law, since the courts usually uphold the status quo unless there are strong reasons for changing it (Eekelaar and Clive, 1977; Eekelaar, 1982). For example, in a fiercely disputed case involving a boy of three, the Court of Appeal ruled that he should remain with his father although his mother was also a caring and competent parent, because the father had demonstrated his ability to look after his son and a change would cause distress to the child (see B *v.* B, reported in *Family Law* 15, 1985, pp. 119). In another case (Re W (A Minor) (Custody) *Family Law* 13, 1983, pp. 47–8) the court ordered that a two-year-old girl who had been happy and well looked after by her father and his cohabitee should live with her mother, although it was recognised that 'the roots of the child were in her father and in his home' (p. 48). The different outcomes in these two cases suggests an assumption on the part of some judges that girls should be brought up by their mothers, while fathers seem to stand a better chance of retaining custody of their sons, in finely balanced cases (Priest and Whybrow, 1986, para. 4.24).

Custody disputes may not be about the children at all: they may be mainly about the occupation of the family home. If parents fear becoming homeless, they may use attack as the best means of defence and allege that the other parent is unfit to have care of the children. This is another variation of the 'innocent or guilty' contest in the divorce itself, with the difference that in custody disputes the court may be expected to decide which is the 'good' parent, with the corollary that the other parent is 'bad', or not good enough to look after the children. The Booth Committee (Report, 1985) said: 'We deplore the situation whereby an order vesting custody in one parent alone can be seen as carrying with it the condemnation of the other parent and the termination of his or her role in the children's lives' (para. 2.27). Apart from the injustice suffered by non-custodial parents who are unreasonably deprived of equal parental status, custody disputes involve loss and damage to the whole family, especially the children. The parent who apparently 'wins' is likely to lose the other parent's co-operation and support and even if custody is settled, there may be long-running access problems or no access at all.

Differences of terminology between the divorce courts and the magistrates' domestic court are confusing for parents and for many social workers too. 'Actual custody' in the domestic court is the equivalent of 'care and control' in the divorce court, though the Matrimonial Causes Act 1973 does not mention the term 'care and control' at all. If there have not been divorce proceedings involving the child, a step-parent or other non-parent with whom a child is living can apply not for 'custody' of the child but for 'custodianship'. The belated introduction of custodianship under section 33 of the Children Act 1975 provides an alternative to adoption by step-parents or by other relatives such as grandparents, but the restrictions on its use make it a much more limited alternative than the Houghton Committee (1972) intended.

Joint custody

The divorce courts, unlike the magistrates' domestic court, can award custody of children to both parents jointly, while generally giving care and control to one parent. Custody, as distinct from care and control, is commonly understood to confer powers relating to a child's education, religion, property and other major decisions, but the legal distinction between sole and joint custody is far from clear. In the case of Dipper *v.* Dipper, Lord Justice Ormrod observed in the Court of Appeal that 'to suggest that a parent with custody dominates the situation so far as education or any other serious matter is concerned is quite wrong' (Law Commission, 1986, para. 2.36). As even the Law Commissioners are uncertain what difference there is between joint and sole custody (Law Commission 1986, para. 2.37), it is not surprising that many social workers are confused by these terms. Parents themselves often think 'custody' means 'care and control' and tend to rely on their solicitor's advice in deciding whether to apply for sole or joint custody.

One of the main arguments for joint custody orders is that they recognise both parents' continuing responsibility for their children, despite the ending of their marriage. These orders can also have considerable symbolic value for children if their meaning can be explained in words the children can understand. Joint custody orders are however the exception rather than the rule, representing only 13 per cent of custody orders made in England and Wales in 1985 (Priest and Whybrow, 1986). Some solicitors advise against joint custody because they think it encourages persistent wrangling between parents, making it harder both for the children and the parents to settle down. There is very little empirical research on the way joint custody works in practice and most of the available research comes from the United States, where joint custody can mean joint physical custody (shared care and control) as well as joint legal custody. Over thirty American states have some form of joint custody statute, though an increasing number distinguish joint physical (residential) custody from joint legal (decision-making) custody (Folberg, 1984). Steinman (1981) found that children and parents generally benefited from joint custody arrangements, provided that the parents were able to accept each other's continuing parental role. The children did not suffer the intense pain of abandonment by a parent but joint physical custody, as opposed to joint legal custody, was stressful for some of them. About a third felt overburdened by the emotional and practical demands of moving constantly between two homes and being scrupulously fair to both parents. Younger children tended to get confused and adolescents needed more freedom for their own friendships and activities. Some English judges take the view that shared care and control of children after divorce is 'positively dangerous' (Priest and Whybrow, 1986, para. 5.34). In a recent case in which an 8-year-old girl spent alternate weeks with each of her divorced parents, the Court of Appeal said that the arrangement was '*prima facie* wrong', although it had worked for five years with no apparent detriment to the child (see Appeal Court decision in R *v.* R, *Times Law Reports*, 28 May 1986).

The Law Commission's recent Review of Child Custody Law (1986) reveals very divergent views on joint custody among judges and enormous variations between courts in making joint or sole custody orders. In 1985, 42 per cent of custody orders in Truro were for joint custody, compared with 30 per cent in Maidstone, 8 per cent in Colchester and 4 per cent in Romford (Priest and Whybrow, 1986). Differences on this scale seem to be beyond all rhyme or reason. Scottish judges are not even sure whether they have the power to order joint custody or not (Seale, 1984) and in a survey of 745 Scottish divorces there were no joint custody orders at all. Dr Eric Clive of the Scottish Law Commission has stated that Scottish divorce courts definitely can award joint custody (quoted Seale, 1984, Annex 2). The reality is that they do not. In England and Wales, the Law Commission (1986) is proposing a fundamental reform of child custody law on the basis that court orders should be 'child-centred' rather than 'parent-centred' (para. 4.49d). The Commission suggests that 'it may be a mistake to see custody, care and control as differently-sized bundles of powers and responsibilities in a descending hierarchy of importance' (para. 4.51) and questions whether any order is necessary if parents can agree arrangements between themselves. Instead of divisive orders allocating custody, care and control to one parent and access to the other, the Commission proposes that parental responsibility should 'run with the child' on a time-sharing basis. Where necessary, the court can be asked to define the frequency and duration of visits and the extent to which parental responsibility should be shared. Many parents find it impossible to work out these difficult decisions in the midst of divorcing each other. Those who refer a dispute to the court will probably be referred to the court welfare service. Court welfare officers are very concerned to help parents reach agreement and co-operate with each other: few of them think they should simply make factual inquiries on the court's behalf. Before discussing this dual role to help families *and* the court, it may be helpful to look briefly at the way the court welfare officer's role has evolved in recent years.

The role of the welfare officer

The number of inquiries undertaken by the Probation Service in divorce and other civil cases rocketed during the seventies, from 10 717 in 1970 to 20 475 in 1980 and 25 000 in 1985 (James and Wilson, 1983; probation Statistics 1985). Civil work comes however at the bottom of the Home Office's (1984) list of priorities for the Probation Service, which called merely for a 'reappraisal of methods' so that 'the existing or a slightly reduced level of resources [can be used] to better effect' (para. VII). 'Better effect' in Home Office terms means helping courts settle contested cases more quickly and cheaply. It does not seem to mean helping families more effectively. It is therefore all the more striking, considering the heavy load on welfare officers and the low status given to civil work, that the last ten years have seen a 'dramatic renaissance of civil work as the source of professional satisfaction, initiative and controversy' (Stone, 1986, p. 38). Many regions of the Probation Service have formed specialist civil work teams and the opportunity to specialise has stimulated fresh thinking and a critical reassessment of traditional approaches. One senior welfare officer (Pearce, 1985), reviewing his nine years' experience of civil work, has observed that 'problems . . . caused by family breakdown are not only more numerous than some years ago but far more complex and certainly more volatile. The creation of units which deal exclusively with civil matters has provided conditions which give much greater insight into the complexity of these problems' (p. 304).

The role of the court welfare officer is not a static one and its evolution reflects the changes that have taken place in social attitudes towards marriage and divorce and the state's responsibilities for children. When police court missionaries were first involved in the magistrates' courts at the end of the nineteenth century, they tended to discourage women from seeking separation even from a violent husband, reconciliation being one of their prime objectives (Murch, 1980). In the course of this century, with easier and greatly increased access to divorce, concerns to protect children rather than marriage have come increasingly to the fore. Following the recommendations of the Denning Committee (1947) and the Morton Commission (1956), probation committees were required to assign probation officers to the divorce court, to report to the court on custody and access issues and generally on the welfare of the children. The focus of the welfare officer's role thus shifted from informal reconciliation counselling to formal inquiries concerning children. It is now in the midst of a further transition from marriage-saving and 'child-saving' to what might be called 'family-saving', since there is usually an explicit concern to help divorcing parents maintain their joint responsibilities as parents, despite the ending of their marriage.

This shift of focus towards helping parents reach joint decisions, rather than assessing their competing rights and claims, is reflected in changes of practice. The traditional approach of interviewing each parent separately and evaluating their rival claims tends to encourage harmful competition between parents who are aware that the judge may follow the welfare officer's recommendations. 'The dirty linen is pegged out in full; the divorce court welfare officer recoils from the onslaught from both sides . . .; he writes a long report about everything; there is a long hearing, the court adjudicates, everyone suffers' (Francis and Shaw, 1981, p. 71). Welfare officers are increasingly questioning the traditional go-between role, but the introduction of new ways of working has led to some sharp clashes between those who defend the 'old' methods and those who champion new ones. Different theoretical approaches and styles of working can lead to arguments between professionals which mirror the uncertainty and conflicts of divorcing parents. Few would dispute that children's welfare is best promoted by parental agreement and from this it can be argued that the welfare officer's main objective should be to facilitate agreement between parents. These 'rose-tinted' assumptions have been questioned however by some experienced officers (Pugsley and Wilkinson, 1984, p. 90), who fear that basic principles of childcare and child protection may be cast aside too lightly. Eekelaar (1985) has argued forcefully that the identification of children's rights with parental autonomy is a dangerous doctrine from the child's point of view, since it can result in social workers focusing solely on parents' perceptions, without giving enough attention to the children. As previously explained, this book is not attempting to deal with the problems of actual or possible child abuse, where an altogether different level of investigation is called for. The concern here is how to help the large numbers of separated and divorcing couples who are reliable, caring and committed parents caught up in personal conflict. Many of these parents can be helped through family meetings designed to facilitate negotiation and joint decision-making, as in the following case.

Case study – the Wilkins family

Mike and Pat Wilkins, a divorcing couple in their early thirties who had been married about eight years, were fighting over the custody, care and control of their two children, Sharon aged 7 and Tom aged 5. Pat had filed a divorce petition based on Mike's 'unreasonable behaviour' and the court adjourned the divorce proceedings and called for a welfare inquiry. Both parents were still living with the children in the matrimonial home and the welfare officer asked them to come to his office to talk about the difficulties, to see how far they could be sorted out through informal discussion. It emerged during the initial discussion that Mike was threatening Pat with a cross-petition alleging that she was involved in a lesbian relationship and unfit to have custody of the children. Pat was terrified this would result in her losing them completely. The welfare officer asked Mike in front of Pat whether he had any cause to think the children were being harmed in any way. Mike said Pat had always been a good mother and he had no complaints so far but he was afraid what might happen if her friend moved in with her. The officer underlined this positive acknowledgement from Mike and it then emerged that Pat did almost all the caring of the children as Mike's hobby was long-distance cycling and he was often away with his mates at weekends. Pat's woman friend turned out to be a kind of red rag that Mike was waving because he did not want to move out and be the loser. The conflict seemed to stem from each parent's fear of total loss and their anxiety to remain in the matrimonial home. Physical custody of the children was not the real issue as Mike did not want to take this on.

By focusing on how they could continue to share the parenting of the children instead of fighting for sole possession, the welfare officer helped Mike and Pat recognise that the children needed a father and a mother and that this was still possible, despite the accusations which they hurled at each other initially. Mike's fears were reframed as deep concern to be involved in the children's lives instead of being pushed out of the family physically and emotionally. Discussions then became less heated, turning to whether they could afford to run two separate households and whether Pat could continue her part-time job to ease the family's tight budget. Sharon and Tom came to the second meeting with their parents and it was very evident from their reactions that they loved both of them and that they badly needed reassurance that neither parent was going to disappear. Mike decided finally that Pat should stay in the family home with the children, and their solicitors negotiated a settlement which preserved Mike's share in the property until the time came for it to be sold. The welfare officer filed a short report explaining that the parents were asking for joint custody, with Pat having care and control of the children and Mike having regular access, including staying access alternate weekends. Consent orders were subsequently made on this basis and a contested court hearing was avoided.

Mike and Pat were helped by joint discussions which focused on their decisions for the future, rather than on past grievances in the marriage. They had got caught up in fighting for the children and the home but as they were basically caring parents, with mutual concern not to injure their children, the welfare officer helped them recognise that some trust was still possible and that there were ways of managing which they had not previously considered. When Mike and Pat found that they could talk to each other and co-operate as parents, they no longer needed the court to make their decisions for them. The early stage at which the welfare officer became involved, the absence of significant third parties and the parents' concern for their children were important positive factors. However, a less structured approach from a worker who got pulled into the parents' conflict and confusion, talking with each of them on their own and conveying angry messages between them, might not have mobilised their own capacity to solve their problems.

Mediating between private and public decision-making

Social workers and welfare officers are often called on to mediate between parents, families or several generations in the same family. They also act as mediators in a broader institutional context between the family's private decision-making system and the public system of judicial decisions in the courts. In this organisational context, the worker may buttress the family system through a period of crisis and change, reducing the court's intrusion to the minimum needed to validate parents' agreements. In the past, welfare officers and social workers were probably more willing to act as agents of statutory authority and control than they are today. Many are now questioning the nature and use of their authority, arguing that a system which allows parents to abdicate their authority to the court perpetuates the problems which caused them to approach the court in the first place. Shuttling backwards and forwards between hostile parents can be enormously time-consuming. Travelling time – and financial cost – can be saved by inviting families to come to office-based meetings in which more intensive work can be done in a shorter time. There are considerable pressures and constraints, however, in working in this way and it is questionable whether the inquiry task can be carried out adequately in a short, 'one-off' family meeting. Assessments may be made hastily, without sufficiently detailed inquiry and discussion, and some very distressed parents and children may not get the individual attention which may be needed as well as working with the family as a whole.

Assessment

In the case of the Wilkins family, the officer focused on the following questions (the numbers do not indicate priority):

1. How much agreement was there between the parents? Were disagreements partly due to lack of information or misunderstandings? If so, the first task was to give relevant information and help clear up misunderstandings.

2. Did both parents seem concerned about their children and anxious to do their best for them? Parenting capacity may be temporarily diminished during a major crisis and a single meeting during this crisis may give misleading impressions. But it should provide at least preliminary indications of relationships and interactions which help plan whether further work is needed with the family and if so, what form it should take.

3. How far were the parents able to differentiate the children's needs from their own and to separate the parental relationship from the marital one? These are very difficult tasks and the stage parents have reached is affected by the length of time since their physical separation and the extent to which they have disengaged emotionally from each other. Some parents need extended help to cope with overwhelming feelings of anger and loss and in some cases a matrimonial supervision order or other help may be needed (see Chapter 6) to continue the work begun by the welfare officer.

4. How did the children relate to their parents and other members of the family? Children's needs and fears may be expressed in non-verbal behaviour, whether or not they can articulate them verbally. As suggested in Chapter 3, a variety of techniques adapted to different ages and stages of development can be used to explore children's feelings and perceptions. It is important also to take account of siblings' relationships with each other and with other key figures – grandparents, step-parents, step-siblings, aunts and uncles.

5. How did each parent view existing and proposed arrangements? What did they see as the main advantages or disadvantages of the alternatives available? In the heat and chaos of separating from each other, parents may make demands which they have not always thought through. The worker can act as an 'agent of reality', asking pragmatic questions which help parents consider what their proposals might actually involve in practice.

6. Who was controlling the time-scale for decisions – one parent, both parents, solicitors, the court? The appropriateness of this time-scale needs to be looked at from the children's point(s) of view, as well as from each parent's

point of view. Children may need decisions without delay about who is going to look after them, so that they can begin to settle down. Parents, however, may want to postpone painful changes as long as possible. Adults and children experience time very differently and young children may have difficulty grasping what 'next week' or 'next month' mean. Time can be a decisive factor in custody decisions as courts tend to uphold the status quo, and so one parent may use stalling tactics to increase the advantage of *de facto* custody. Welfare officers therefore need to guard against manipulation by a parent to prolong their work in a way that strengthens this parent's position. In some apparently hopeless situations the worker may be relieved to give up, but there are also strong pressures to struggle on, and these pressures are often within the worker as well as outside. Persuading oneself that progress is possible or just beginning can be an emotional defence against acknowledging defeat. If a welfare officer's work with a family in the context of a welfare inquiry shows signs of becoming prolonged, the reasons for carrying on should be discussed with a supervisor and/or colleagues (see Chapter 7), as the worker's involvement may be effectively maintaining the family's problems.

7. How much conflict was there in the family, how was it being expressed and what was its function? The extent to which children and other family members are caught up in the conflict needs to be considered in deciding how to structure sessions – who should be involved and at what stage – and in planning the agenda for each session. Disputes over money or the occupation of the home often fuel conflicts over custody or access. If several issues are interrelated with each other, parents may need help in disentangling these issues and recognising the underlying connections between them.

8. Were there particular problems such as physical illness or depression which might be affecting a parent's ability to take decisions? If so, referral to and/or liaison with other agencies may be indicated (see the section on networking in Chapter 7).

9. Was there a risk of fitting the family to a preconceived

theory and missing its unique characteristics? Might the worker's own values – with regard to lesbianism, for example – influence the outcome? Or might cultural factors be overlooked which affect the parent's decisions and attitudes?

10. Does any information or first-hand observations of the parents and children together ring alarm bells that the children are at risk or in need of care which the parents themselves are unable to provide? If so, further investigation and appropriate action are obviously necessary, to avoid or reduce the risk to the children.

Intractable conflict

Families like the Wilkins can be rewarding to work with because they respond to the help that is offered and begin relating to each other with more trust. These families help beleaguered workers cope with the fatigue, depression and frustration thay are often left with by families who may be at the other end of the continuum of difficulty. An experienced American mediator (Ricci, 1986) has suggested that some parents are 'hostility junkies' who have become addicted to fighting as a means of survival. These couples are extremely difficult to help. They may resent the welfare officer as an authority figure acting on the court's behalf, and the court may criticise the officer for delaying decisions about the children with fruitless attempts to solve the parent's problems. The unfortunate welfare officer may feel under attack from all sides and be understandably anxious to get out of the 'hot seat' as soon as possible.

In one such family, the Murrays, the parents' uncontrolled hostility and grief swamped the welfare officer's attempts to help them. The father, Colin, would weep, plead and argue with rising hysteria until the mother, Alison exploded at him as on many previous occasions. They had already been to marriage guidance and Colin had also seen a psychotherapist, but each professional who intervened was discarded in turn. Every single issue was fought over – the divorce itself, custody, access, the matrimonial home and money. There were also huge rows over issues which could be seen as symbolic, such as a painting which Alison sold to raise money for herself and the children. She and Colin seemed to need to fight each other as a way of holding on to a vulnerable and fragile sense of identity. Colin was close to collapse and talked of committing suicide. A very poignant factor in the conflict was the stillbirth of their first child twelve years earlier and the parents' inability to mourn the loss of this first child together.

Instead of discussing at greater length the problems of this deeply unhappy family, it may be more helpful to identify the positive factors which helped the officer hold to her task without becoming totally overwhelmed and demoralised. These included good support from colleagues and seniors (see Chapter 7); good working relationships with both parents' solicitors; and clarity about the nature of the task, despite its unsuperable difficulties. For example, when Colin enraged Alison with derogatory remarks about Stan, her boyfriend, the officer barred Stan as a subject for discussion. As Stan had little contact with the children, the officer suggested that Colin and Alison should not allow their feelings about Stan to dominate their decisions as parents. In this way they were brought back to 'here and now' questions about the next access visit and how it could be managed with minimum upset for the children. Colin and Alison's personal suffering was still acute, but they perhaps managed the practicalities of the next seven days fractionally better. A very limited agenda focusing on the children's immediate needs and feelings helped contain the situation, even though little improvement was visible.

There is of course no single right way of working with conflicted families and the pressures to find solutions can be very great. A clearly defined but flexible model of work, placed in a particular theoretical framework, can increase clarity and confidence. However, the choice of one model implies the rejection of others and this can lead to doors being closed, literally or metaphorically, if different teams or agencies reject each other's approach.

Different approaches to the inquiry task

James and Wilson (1983) found in their survey of civil work practice that nearly all probation officers favoured an active, interventionist role with the aim of improving communication in families and reducing conflict. Just over half the officers who responded said they worked within a particular theoretical framework and 17 per cent (the largest single group) referred to family therapy. There was evidence however of substantial variations of practice, particularly with regard to involving children. Half the officers (49 per cent) said they never talked with children of five and under, whereas 45 per cent sometimes did so and 6 per cent always did. 41 per cent said they always contacted social services, compared with 59 per cent who sometimes did so. Some regularly contacted the police, others did not.

Practice with regard to report-writing and recommendations to the court was also very varied, some officers being prepared to make specific recommendations while others offered their interpretations of the family's difficulties without giving an opinion one way or another. The National Association of Probation Officers (NAPO, 1984) discourages recommendations which feed into the adversarial system, arguing that 'in the absence of risk to the child, it is both arrogant and inappropriate to make value judgements about what usually amounts to different styles of parenting' (p. 1). The courts have made it clear however that it is essential for welfare officers to observe how children relate to each parent. In a case in which a father had looked after his baby daughter for eighteen months after the mother left home, the welfare officer concerned was criticised by judges in the Court of Appeal for failing to see the mother and child together (see the case of Edwards *v*. Edwards, in *Family Law*, 16, 1986, pp. 99–100). The Court also directed that if a report contains second-hand information, the officer must indicate its source and explain why the information has been accepted.

Problems may also arise as a result of the different perspectives and professional training of lawyers and social workers. The parties' solicitors may expect the report to give factual descriptions of each party's accommodation, number of bedrooms and so on. Welfare officers (Shepherd and Howard, 1985a) may see little value in this type of reporting, arguing that home visits are usually irrelevant as a basis for family assessments because material conditions in the home are rarely so bad as to prevent a child living in or visiting that home. Unfortunately, adversarial legal traditions may encourage parents to accuse each other of neglecting or harming the children as a weapon to win a custody or access battle. When these weapons are brandished in a sensational way, professionals may be persuaded to focus on the weapon rather than on the battle itself. An officer who gets caught in assessing which of two physical environments is better for the child, without helping the parents resolve this contest themselves, may fail to protect the child from the psychological harm of continued warfare.

If parents are interviewed separately, it can be very difficult for welfare officers to reconcile their conflicting versions of the same events. Their contradictory statements may seem like fragmented snapshots taken from different angles – fragments which do not form a coherent picture when they are put together. Cantwell (1986) observed that the tendency to interview parents and children separately and to think of them as individuals rather than as a family undergoing a process of change is a little like watching one cricketer at a time instead of viewing the whole match. 'Quite distorted and value-laden conclusions have sometimes been drawn from essentially fragmentary evidence' (p. 279). It must be acknowledged, however, that if welfare officers lack sufficient insight and skills, distorted and value-laden conclusions could also be drawn from family meetings.

Welfare inquiries, conciliation and mediation

There has been heated debate in recent years as to whether welfare officers who invite both parents to come to family meetings with their children, using a settlement-seeking approach, are practising 'conciliation' or not (Davis, 1983, 1985; Taylor, 1984; Shepherd and Howard, 1985b). Clearly, welfare officers and conciliators in independent services share common objectives and may use similar methods of working (Parkinson, 1986a). The Booth Committee (1985) recognised that welfare officers often help parents reach agreement and acknowledged that 'assistance of this kind can be of considerable value' (para. 4.62). The Committee stressed however that there are essential differences between the role of conciliator and that of the welfare officer who makes a report to the court. Conciliators are not empowered to make assessments on the court's behalf. Their contract is solely with the parties and not with the court, even where the court initiates the referral. Many parents need a private forum where they can talk about decisions and practical arrangements, without fear that what they say could somehow be used to discredit them if their case goes to court. Conciliation needs to be understood from the outset as a legally privileged process which neither party nor the conciliator can exploit to benefit one party, by including in evidence to the court prejudicial statements made – or allegedly made – during conciliation. Without this privilege, conciliators could be called as a witness by one or both parties and involved in further arguments in court over what was said during conciliation. The privilege attaching to conciliation can be waived with both parties' consent and it can be overridden by a conciliator or by the court if a child is thought to be at risk.

A recent Direction from the Principal Divorce Registry of the Family Division (1986) distinguished conciliation from welfare inquiries as follows:

A Judge or Registrar, before ordering an enquiry or report by a Court Welfare Officer, should, where local conciliation facilities exist, consider whether the case is a suitable one for attempts to be made to settle any of the issues by the conciliation process. . . . If conciliation fails, any report which is ordered must be made by an officer who did not act as a conciliator. Where the court directs an enquiry and report by a Welfare Officer, it is the function of the Welfare Officer, to assist the court by investigating the circumstances of the child, or children, concerned and the important figures in their lives, to report what he sees and hears, to offer the court his assessment of the situation and, where appropriate to make a recommendation. In such circumstances, it is not the role of the Welfare Officer to attempt conciliation although he may encourage the parties to settle their differences if the likelihood of a settlement arises during the course of his enquiries.

(Registrar's Direction, 28 July 1986).

Much of the confusion that has arisen about welfare officers practising conciliation has stemmed from confusion over terminology rather than from fundamental disagreements of principle. Of course welfare officers should encourage parents to agree and co-operate with each other and family meetings may be the most effective way of enabling them to agree. Jackson (1986) suggests that a settlement-seeking approach in the context of a welfare inquiry should be called 'mediation', not 'conciliation', so that similar methods of working can be used without confusing the welfare officer's role with that of conciliator. The welfare officer acts on the court's behalf and has a statutory responsibility to report all relevant information to the court, especially where the welfare of children is concerned. He or she may need to contact social services and other agencies, teachers and other adults with direct responsibility for the children. The extent of the inquiry must depend on the circumstances of each case and on the ability of both parents to work out their own solutions, with the welfare officer's help.

It is ironic that well-intentioned efforts to settle parental disputes sometimes cause conflict between the professionals involved. There have been some clashes between High Court judges and court welfare officers who have tried to combine conciliation with the preparation of a welfare report without apparently managing either function adequately (Ewbank, 1985). In some areas there are tensions around the control of court welfare work and it is certainly debatable how far one discipline (the law) should direct another (social work) how to exercise its professional skills. On the other hand, statutory duties and responsibilities cannot be rewritten by welfare officers and social workers, however committed they are to helping families. In a recent case it was established in court that a liaison divorce court welfare officer does not have discretion to allocate a welfare inquiry to a local authority social worker responsible for supervising a child of the family (see the case of Andrew *v.* Andrew, Plymouth County Court, November 1985). The divorce court alone must authorise the appointment of the reporting officer.

National guide-lines on court welfare work are to be issued shortly by the Civil Work Sub-Committee of the Association of Chief Officers of Probation, but it remains to be seen how far they will produce a unified approach across the country. It is essential that welfare officers, social workers and voluntary conciliators fully understand the legal context in which they work and that they explain to families whether their discussions are confidential or reportable to the court. New approaches to court welfare work have been greeted with enthusiasm and commitment. But before plunging into the maelstrom of family conflict with new professional flippers acquired from family therapy and/or conciliation, we need to be clear whether the limits of the water we swim in are controlled by the family, or by the court and its officers. In the following chapter, conciliation and mediation practice is explored further with reference to various models of co-working and conflict management techniques which may be helpful in a wide range of social work contexts.

5

Conflict Management and Conciliation

Conflict is generally assumed to be destructive, but life devoid of conflict would indeed be sterile. Conflict has positive as well as negative elements and instead of being avoided or suppressed it needs to be seen as a dynamic force whose energy can be harnessed in active problem-solving (Deutsch, 1973; Folberg and Taylor, 1984). Social workers encounter many different kinds of personal, family and social conflict and there is increasing awareness that conflict management skills require more than goodwill, common sense and a few soothing words here and there. At a theoretical level, conciliators and mediators utilise concepts drawn from a number of sources, including systems theory and family therapy, conflict theory, crisis theory and attachment theory. Conciliation needs to forge links between these theoretical frameworks in developing a distinctive theoretical base of its own: it should not be just a social work hotpot from which ideas and methods are picked out at random and swallowed whole. Conciliators need to articulate and adhere to a consistent body of theory and principle, whilst retaining sufficient flexibility to adapt to the needs of individual families.

Conciliation and mediation

Interest in conflict management techniques has been greatly stimulated in Britain in the last decade by what might be called 'the conciliation movement'. Conciliation and mediation have a long history in many cultures: many societies across the world have developed peaceful methods of settling disputes between individuals, families or tribal groups, using neutral third parties who help disputants negotiate mutually acceptable solutions. Conciliation as a method of settling disputes associated with divorce is however a relatively recent development. In the early Conciliation Courts which were set up in the United States before the Second World War, conciliation was synonymous with reconciliation and couples on the brink of divorce were often persuaded to remain together instead of divorcing. Gradually, as divorce became more common and socially acceptable, reconciliation counselling was no longer seen as the primary objective and court counsellors increasingly helped divorcing couples negotiate joint decisions, particularly over arrangements for their children.

The Finer Committee on One-parent Families (1974) called for a new, unified family court in England and Wales in which conciliation would be used as far as possible instead of litigation to settle disputes and encourage co-operation between divorcing parents. The Finer Report (1974) distinguished 'reconciliation' – re-uniting the parties – from 'conciliation', defined as 'assisting the parties to deal with the consequences of the established breakdown of their marriage, whether resulting in a divorce or a separation, by reaching agreements or giving consents or reducing the area of conflict upon custody, support, access to and education of the children – and every other matter which calls for a decision on future arrangements' (para. 4.288). Although shelved by successive governments, the Finer Committee's recommendations drew an active response from many professionals across the country. Small groups of probation officers, lawyers, social workers and others began to plan locally based conciliation schemes which would take referrals from the court and from solicitors and parents themselves, to help parents work out agreed decisions instead of asking the court to arbitrate between them. Although many parents agree about their children without outside help, others need help at different stages of the divorce process and for varying amounts of time. Some respond to short-term help on a voluntary basis before they start formal legal proceedings, whereas others accept help only through the court's intervention. Both the timing and the method of intervention may be crucial. Follow-up research in other countries suggests that early, pre-court conciliation is associated with improved co-operation and easier relationships between parents, compared with interventions made during or after divorce proceedings. Evidence of the advantages of early conciliation is given in a report from Frontenac, Ontario, Canada (1984) (see Chapter 7).

Organisational settings for conciliation

There are at least six organisational settings in which conciliation is currently being practised in Britain:

1. In-court conciliation is undertaken by court welfare officers in the context of conciliation appointments arranged by the court. In many divorce county courts, the Principal Divorce Registry in London and some domestic courts, couples who are contesting custody, access or the divorce itself attend appointments before a registrar, judge, or magistrates' clerk. With the help of the parties' solicitors, the issues in dispute are clarified and the parties themselves are then invited to withdraw with a welfare officer who acts as a conciliator, not as an investigator for the court. If agreement is reached in the course of a short discussion (only about forty minutes in some courts), consent orders may be made on the spot. If no agreement is reached, the case may be adjourned for further conciliation or for a welfare inquiry. The Probation Statistics for 1985 reported that 13 000 referrals for conciliation were undertaken by probation officers in that year. In 6000 cases, conciliation was completed in the divorce court during the hearing, while 5000 required an adjournment. Similarly, about half the 2000 conciliation cases undertaken in the magistrates' domestic court were completed in court.

2. Conciliation schemes are also organised by civil work units of the probation service, without the court's direct in-

volvement. Marriage guidance counsellors or other volunteers may be recruited to co-work with members of the
civil work team and conciliation generally takes place out
of court. However, as Davis (1982) and Roberts (1983)
have pointed out, it can be difficult for welfare officers to
lay aside their statutory authority and in some schemes
there has been confusion about the workers' role in
relation to the family and the court. This form of conciliation is usually limited to one or two meetings per case.

3. Independent conciliation services have been set up in
England, Wales and Scotland and the Irish Republic as
autonomous agencies under the control of a newly consti-
tuted management committee. A few pilot schemes are
funded by central government but most have to glean
funds laboriously from a range of sources. These services
complement court-connected schemes by offering help to
unmarried, married and divorced couples at all stages of
separation and divorce. Referrals are taken from solicitors, the parties themselves, other agencies and in some
areas from the courts as well. One independent service
takes referrals in court from the registrar but this is
unusual. Most services are based in the community and
some accept walk-in referrals. Access to children is the
most common issue but there is often conflict on other
issues as well. Two to three appointments per case
(occasionally more) are spaced over a period of several
weeks or months, depending on the pace of work that
seems appropriate.

4. Conciliation projects are also run under the wing of large
national charities and therapeutic institutions, such as Dr
Barnardo's (projects in Liverpool and Tunbridge Wells),
the Children's Society (North Devon), the National Children's Home (Bury, Lancs.), Marriage Guidance (North-
umberland and Tyneside) and the Institute for Family
Therapy (London). Conciliation in these settings may be
influenced to some extent by the parent organisation but
boundaries are maintained between different agency functions, so that conciliation is distinguished from other forms
of help such as therapy, counselling and child welfare
work.

5. Some services cater specifically for couples from a particular ethnic or religious background, such as the Asian
   Family Conciliation Service in Birmingham and the Jewish
   Family Mediation Service in London. The Asian service
   offers conciliation to Asian couples and families and at
   another level it mediates between Asian and western
   cultural traditions. Asian community leaders are sometimes directly involved and the service liaises with West
   Midlands Probation Service and other agencies. Useful
   guide-lines on divorce court welfare work with Asian
   families, *Asian Marriages and the Welfare Services*, have
   been prepared by West Midlands Probation Service and
   Link House Council Consultancy Group. The staff of the
   Birmingham service speak five Asian languages between
   them and help bridge the gap between different Asian
   cultures and English legal and welfare systems, while
   maintaining the confidentiality which is fundamental to
   the conciliation process.

   To date there are no comparable special services for
   West Indian and black African families and I am aware of
   only one black conciliator in one of the independent
   services. Some services see a substantial number of black
   families but little is known so far about their experience of
   conciliation. Conciliators who work with black families
   need to be knowledgeable about black family patterns and
   particularly about shared child care as practised in Africa,
   the Caribbean and many parts of Asia. Black parents may
   be less inclined than white parents to claim sole ownership
   of children and they are not criticised if they entrust their
   children to others who can offer them a more stable home.
   On the contrary, this is normally seen as a caring and
   responsible decision on their part (Loftus, 1986).

6. Most services are staffed by conciliators with a social work
   or counselling background but some use volunteers without any formal training. A small experiment in interdisciplinary conciliation has recently started in London in
   which a conciliator with social work and family conciliation experience co-works with one of a number of
   solicitors. The solicitors have had training in conciliation
   and do not act as legal advisers to either party. Couples are

helped to negotiate and reach agreement on all issues relating to their separation or divorce, including financial and property matters.

National Family Conciliation Council

Most of the independent and semi-independent conciliation services are affiliated to the National Family Conciliation Council (NFCC), a voluntary organisation with charitable status which seeks to co-ordinate these otherwise ad hoc developments. By October 1986, 34 services were fully affiliated, 6 provisionally affiliated, 9 associated and another 30 in various stages of development. The NFCC promotes good professional standards in the practice of conciliation, setting criteria for affiliation and helping services with organisational issues and training. A major task has been the formulation of a Code of Practice for conciliators, in consultation with the Law Society and the Solicitors' Family Law Association. It is important to establish ground-rules regarding written and verbal communications between solicitors, conciliators, their clients, other agencies and the courts, to reduce confusion and possible abuse of the process. The term 'conciliation' tends to be used ambiguously to refer both to general objectives and specific methods of work (James and Wilson, 1986), and its principles of voluntary participation, confidentiality and party control are easily infringed, especially if conciliators are used to working in a statutory setting (Davis and Bader, 1985). The NFCC's Code of Practice (1986) defines the principles of conciliation and lays down ground-rules regarding 'without prejudice' communications with solicitors and the limits to confidentiality in relation to children at risk.

The boundaries of conciliation

Questions are often asked about the boundaries between conciliation and counselling, and between conciliation and family therapy (Parkinson, 1985, 1986b). There is inevitably some degree of overlap between these processes but there are also important differences which need to be thought through. Conciliation by definition must involve both parties and with their consent, children and other family members may take part as well. Conciliators encourage parents to reach consensual decisions for the future which generally have legal as well as social and emotional consequences for the family as a whole. Divorce counselling, on the other hand, often involves only one partner, offering help with personal distress and adjustment, and generally has no formal links with the legal process of divorce. Conciliators do not usually explore perceptions, feelings and past history to the extent that a counsellor or therapist may do. Conciliation is characterised by its brevity and intensity and by the difficulties of balancing the discordant needs and views of those involved. Although limited in time and scope, it may none the less influence family interaction at a deeper level, by enabling parents to listen to each other and helping them focus on their children's feelings.

Researchers in the Conciliation Project Unit based at the University of Newcastle embarked in September 1985 on a three-year evaluative study of different conciliation schemes, examining their scope, methods, costs and their effectiveness from the consumer point of view. The researchers (Walker and Wray, 1986) have pointed out that the assumed dichotomy between in-court and out-of-court services is an over-simplification and that the court's involvement is a major variable both in statutory and voluntary schemes. Conciliators in fully independent services do not have any formal authority and parents may think they 'lack teeth'. Court welfare officers inevitably carry some of the court's authority, and they have 'clout' as the agents of a powerful institution which has its own interest in settling disputes. Conciliators may therefore combine two different kinds of power: formal authority derived from the court and/or the professional authority which is necessary to contain conflict and balance unequal bargaining positions. This combination of institutional and professional authority may seem formidable to some families, and conciliators need self-control and skill to refrain from arbitrating, especially when parents appeal to them to do so.

Conciliation is increasingly recognised as a structured method of working which calls for interdisciplinary knowledge and skills, applied within a clearly defined context. Its practice is stimulating fresh thinking about conflict management in general and specifically about ways of working with families split by separation or divorce. These innovatory developments are influencing work in statutory services in two main ways: first, in emphasising the value of continued shared parenting after separation or divorce, and secondly in popularising certain models of working, such as co-working. Much of this learning can be applied in other social work contexts but the context must be kept firmly in mind when methods are borrowed from one process and applied to another.

Imbalances in conciliation

Conflicts over custody and access arrangements inevitably affect children. Grandparents, step-parents, new partners and children from other relationships may be closely involved as well. It can be very difficult for a single worker to avoid alignments and keep track of all the interactions that are taking place. First, there is the task of engaging two or more people who may be very disturbed by each other' s presence. Secondly, there is the problem of absorbing and responding to a great deal of information which is typically presented in confused and highly emotional terms, both verbally and non-verbally. Thirdly, there is the problem of unequal bargaining power, a term derived from negotiations in commercial and industrial disputes to denote the imbalance of resources between the two main protagonists – material, emotional, psychological and/or their support from third parties. Very often, one parent is negotiating from a position of strength while the other is struggling to gain a toe-hold. The parent who has physical custody of the children has a strong advantage in custody proceedings, as the court generally upholds the status quo. The custodial parent is also in a strong position to control how much access takes place, even where the court makes an order for defined access. A single worker trying to balance these inequalities of power may be drawn into a coalition with the parent who seeks access to the children. On the other hand, a parent who is being subjected to a barrage of demands or threats may urgently need support. In nearly all cases, there is the problem of helping parents to cope with further stressful contact just when one or both of them may be trying to detach themselves emotionally from each other.

Feminists have expressed particular concern that women may be put under pressure by their husbands and by conciliators to accept arrangements contrary to their interests, without receiving adequate legal advice and protection (Bottomley and Olley, 1983). These concerns are based on American experience and they have not so far been substantiated by British research. Unpublished research by Davis and Roberts at Bromley found on the contrary that women who attended Bromley Family Mediation Bureau felt adequately supported and that they particularly valued the presence of two workers, one of whom was male. Moreover, conciliation in Britain, unlike private mediation schemes in the United States, normally takes place in conjunction with separate legal advice to each party (Parkinson, 1986a).

Co-working in conciliation

Co-working in conciliation and mediation can offer a number of advantages, such as greater capacity to contain inequalities of power and strong emotions within families. Two or more workers can offer greater protection and control if physical violence has occurred and this is also safer for the workers themselves, since a solitary worker making home visits can be at serious risk. Advocates of co-working also believe that conciliators who work in a pair or team can respond better to the conflicting needs of different family members, withstanding the pressures which might overwhelm a single worker. The advantages of co-working are not automatic, however: to be effective, it requires more than a belief that two workers are better than one. Ad hoc co-working which relies on intuitive responses and moral support rather than planned interventions contains various pitfalls for the unwary. If co-workers are to work together effectively, they need to plan their approach carefully, taking account of questions such as:

1. Have alternative models of co-working been carefully considered and discussed? Are prospective co-workers equally clear about the theoretical model they intend using and their respective roles within this model?

2. Are there any factors which might interfere with the roles they assign to each other? A less experienced worker paired with a senior colleague may feel inhibited from intervening or disagreeing.

3. Are the workers comfortable with each other's personal style and is there sufficient trust between them? What will happen if they fail to establish rapport with each other and dislike each other's style? Some workers use humour to reduce tension in family meetings but their colleagues may find this inappropriate or insensitive.

4. What about gender? Gender roles are very significant in conflicts arising from separation and divorce. What are the implications of pairing two workers of the same or opposite sex? A separated father is liable to feel threatened in a room with three powerful women (his ex-wife and two female workers) and a divorced mother may need the support of a male worker in confronting a belligerent ex-husband. Each parent may also fear that a worker of the same sex may be 'seduced' by the opposite-sex parent. Researchers (Clulow and Vincent, in press) have found that clients' reactions to workers' gender are stronger than professionals like to think. These feelings are often concealed and it may be necessary to raise the issue of gender explicitly in order to allay suspicions about its influence. For example, an introduction to the first session can help parents feel more at ease by including something on these lines: 'Divorce is so common these days and yet there are no general rules about the way divorced parents are expected to share responsibility for their children and how much help they are entitled to expect from each other. We ourselves (indicating co-worker, where appropriate) don't have any fixed views about this because each

family is different and there are so many different ways of managing things. The fact that we are . . . (male/female) doesn't mean that we look at things only from the woman's point of view or only from the man's point of view and we hope neither of you will find that we take sides. If you do feel this, it would help us if you could say so.' The worker who says this should make eye contact with each parent and check that each responds.

5. Has enough time been scheduled before and after each session to plan the approach and review it afterwards? Anticipating problems increases confidence in handling them. As colleagues get used to working together, they should find it progressively easier to communicate in shorthand, without needing to discuss each point exhaustively as they go along.

Different models of co-working

Various forms of co-working are being used in conciliation and mediation and many of these models are influenced by concepts and methods derived from family therapy. Some rely heavily on a particular therapeutic model, such as strategic family therapy, while others incorporate a variety of ideas and techniques from different sources. While recognising the value of these borrowings, it is important to consider how far certain methods of working can be imported from one process (therapy) to another (conciliation) without blurring roles and objectives. Three common models of co-working which are being used by conciliators and court welfare officers are:

1. The partnership model.
2. Live consultation in the room.
3. The Milan method.

1. The partnership model

In its simplest form, co-working consists of a symmetrical partnership between two workers who share the same role, though they may allocate certain tasks to one member of the pair. Co-workers may model ways of negotiating as a means of helping antagonistic couples learn similar methods themselves. But modelling 'successful' ways of relating can increase feelings of inadequacy in observers without the desired learning taking place. There is also the risk of co-workers misunderstanding each other's cues or intentions and a split may develop between them if each worker identifies with one parent rather than responding to the family as a whole.

Many conciliators with experience of working alone and with a partner express a personal preference for co-working. But not enough is yet known about co-working in conciliation to establish with any certainty whether families derive more help from two workers than from one. Parents may be less easily convinced of the benefits of co-working than the workers themselves, and more may depend on the workers' skills than on the model *per se*.

2. *Live consultation in the room*

Family therapists such as Haley (1976) and Papp (1977) found that a co-worker who takes the role of consultant to the therapist may help the therapist gain better understanding of family processes because the consultant's interventions are made from outside the system of therapist-plus-family. The consultant may sit a little further back in order to maintain a certain distance, while the therapist joins with the family to elicit information, clarify issues, etc.

The main advantage of this division of roles in conciliation is that the consultant can focus on processes which may be maintaining particular conflicts in the family, while the conciliator concentrates on gathering factual information and exploring practical alternatives. Families are so complex that it is often difficult for one worker to combine these two functions. Parents may appreciate the need for an additional worker whose role is to keep discussions on track, underline things that may have been missed and suggest fresh perspectives or a new way forward. The consultant can also notice and reflect on contradictions between parents' professed concerns and their actual behaviour or tone of voice, drawing the conciliator's attention to this if appropriate. Examples of interventions the consultant may make in conciliation include the following (adapted from Smith and Kingston, 1980 p. 381–3):

(a) pointing to an issue which the conciliator has not recognised or responded to (e.g. the effect of an unresolved dispute over maintenance on each parent's feelings about access).

(b) picking up an important statement which does not seem to have been heard (e.g. 'I'm not trying to stop the children seeing you') and asking the conciliator to find out if the other parent can accept this reassurance.

(c) lowering the temperature by making a normalising statement which the conciliator can take over and expand. ('Mrs . . . seems worried that . . . [child] has reverted to behaviour he/she had previously grown out of, but this often happens for a while after parents split up. Could you ask her what happens when . . .').

(d) deflecting unproductive argument by asking the conciliator to return to a focus that has been lost.

(e) reframing one party's position or behaviour (see the end of this chapter).

(f) pointing to a process that has not been identified by the conciliator (e.g. the way a child is being used as a go-between).

(g) suggesting an option that does not seem to have occurred to either party or the conciliator ('Could you ask Mr and Mrs . . . if there is anyone else they both trust with whom they could leave the children before and after access visits, instead of having to meet each other face to face?').

Live consultation in family therapy generally involves time-out in which the workers withdraw briefly to another room for private consultation. If this happens in conciliation, some parents may feel very anxious about being left alone and certainly one of the main objectives is to encourage open communication between all concerned. Some parents, however, make good use of time on their own, even working out a solution while the conciliators are out of the room!

Kingston and Smith (1983) suggest that live consultation in

family therapy involves six main stages of work, requiring a considerable investment of time and effort by both workers. Conciliation generally has more limited and concrete objectives than family therapy and resources may not allow the use of two workers in every case. It may be feasible however to call on the help of a co-worker in particularly difficult situations, after problems have been identified which seem insuperable to a single conciliator. Parents who are dubious about the value of another appointment may agree to a further meeting if they are offered the help of two workers instead of one, to review their difficulties afresh.

3. The Milan method

The Milan method is a form of strategic and family therapy, so-called because it is based on the work of a group of family therapists in Milan. It is not possible within a few short paragraphs to give an adequate explanation of this model and the way it seeks to chart interrelationships between meaning and behaviour in family systems. (For a full exposition, readers are referred to Palazzoli, Boscolo, Cecchin and Prata 1971, 1980; Palazzoli, 1984, 1985.) The fundamental ethos of the Milan school is that professionals should be objective, neutral and uncommitted to producing change. They should not press families to change patterns of functioning which may have a stabilising or protective function for the family as a whole. Instead, they should offer families a positive connotation of their difficulties which gives them permission to remain the same while indicating the possibility of change. Paradoxically, this may lead to unforced changes of perception and behaviour and thus to improved functioning.

Gorell Barnes (1984, pp. 112–13) summarises those aspects of the Milan model which are most relevant to social workers: the use of a team or partner whose objectivity will be greater than that of the therapist working directly with the family; the team's detachment and neutrality in forming conceptual maps of families and the way they function; and the recognition of the importance of implicit rules governing family behaviour over two or more generations. As Gorell Barnes points out (p. 113), the lack of an explicit change orientation makes the Milan model difficult to use in situations where change is urgently required. Its use in court welfare work and conciliation is therefore controversial, since welfare officers and conciliators are committed to producing some degree of change, by bringing estranged family members together and overcoming blocks to agreement. An uncritical application of the Milan model in mediation and conciliation could encourage a passive acceptance of continuing conflict, without helping parents negotiate actively with each other. Workers using this method tend to adopt a detached stance which some families may find offputting, but the good outcomes reported by practitioners suggest that many conflicted families can be helped by this approach (Howard and Shepherd, 1987). Its use in conciliation and court welfare work does however raise ethical as well as theoretical questions. Haynes (1984) among others has argued that couples who come voluntarily for *conciliation* have the right not to have *therapy* imposed on them without their knowledge and full consent. Shepherd and Howard (1985b) counter this by pointing out that if the workers' comments enable families to *choose* a different pattern of behaviour, then the principle of empowering parents has not been violated.

Techniques derived from strategic therapy, such as circular questioning, hypothesising and paradoxical interventions, can be very helpful both in court-related mediation work and in voluntary conciliation, provided workers understand how to use them appropriately. At an international conference on conciliation organised by the Institute of Family Therapy and held in London in October 1984, Arnon Bentovim demonstrated the use of strategic methods in a role-play in which a separated father was accused by the mother of failing to turn up for access visits regularly. Both parents were startled by the conciliator's suggestion that the father was helping her by being unreliable, because the children then depended wholly on their mother and the mother's management of the children was more secure. The father began to think this through and was less willing to allow the mother to be the only reliable parent. Whether this would have led in real life to more reliable behaviour on his part and greater willingness on the mother's part to share responsibility for the children has to remain a matter for conjecture. Paradoxical messages can be used effectively in conciliation but conciliators should take account of solicitors' probable reactions, as well as those of each parent, as parents may consult with their solicitors and rely on their advice.

Conciliation – basic tasks

Whatever model of conciliation is used, certain basic tasks have to be addressed such as convening couples and families, deciding with them who should be directly involved, gathering relevant facts, containing or pre-empting conflict, exploring options and reframing positions. Haynes (1984) proposes a structured sequence of tasks which he lists as: intake and orientation; fact-finding; problem definition; option development; and bargaining.

At the intake/orientation stage, clear explanations are needed of the conciliation process and the way information will be handled. Follow-up studies exploring clients' experience of social work and counselling (Mayer and Timms, 1970; Maluccio, 1979; Oldfield, 1983; Hunt, 1985) have shown that clients' dissatisfaction is closely associated with workers failing to explain their approach and objectives adequately. Conciliators normally begin by explaining how they work and offering a time-limited contract. The vocabulary they use needs to be adapted to the family's level of crisis and probable comprehension. Many also give parents an explanatory leaflet to take away with them.

Convening hostile parents

Separating and divorcing couples are usually very conscious of the way power is allocated between them, subjectively and objectively (Haynes, 1981; Parkinson, 1986a) and the potential loser in this power struggle may turn to conciliation in the hope that it will tip the scales in his or her favour. The initial stage of convening conjoint or family meetings should therefore be seen as the first stage of conciliation. It needs to be planned with great care to avoid creating coalitions before the central part of the work gets under way. Convening issues familiar to family therapists (Carpenter and Treacher, 1983) are equally relevant in conciliation. Whitaker (1977) suggests that two 'battles' take place in family therapy which he called the 'battle for structure' and the 'battle for initiative'. In conciliation, these battles start when the help-seeking parent tries to enlist the conciliator as a personal ally, rather than as a neutral resource for the family as a whole. Whitaker considers it crucial for the therapist to win these battles by convening the family, rather than just accepting whoever decides to come. Conciliators need to use similar care and skill to engage both parties, where only one is asking for help.

The parent who makes the first approach to a conciliation service often says that there is no point in approaching the other parent, as he or she is bound to be unco-operative. An attempt is thus made to lure the agency into a supportive alliance. If the agency responds with a half-hearted approach to the second parent via the first one, a negative response is predictable if the parents are antagonistic. It is usually preferable to approach the second parent directly or via his or her solicitor, emphasising that help is equally available to both parents and that appointments can be arranged only if both agree to come.

In the case of Mr and Mrs Johnson, who were on the verge of taking an access dispute to court, it was important to be able to write to Mr Johnson: 'I only spoke to Mrs Johnson for a few minutes when she phoned and so I know extremely little about the situation. In fact I asked her not to start explaining her side of things to me as I would much rather hear about it from both of you together. I think a joint discussion would be useful to help me understand how each of you sees the present situation and what you think could be done to make it easier both for you and the children. Would you be able to come to see me . . . (place, date, time)? If this is possible for you, I will see if Mrs Johnson can manage the same time.' Mr Johnson said later that he would have refused to come if he thought his name had been blackened before he had had a chance to give his side of the story.

In another case, a very distraught mother was afraid that she would lose face in front of her husband by breaking down in tears. The intake worker sought to reduce this fear by saying that men as well as women often cry during painful discussions and that the partner who does not cry may also be very upset. A husband in another case sounded very truculent when he phoned in reply to a letter offering him an appointment. He became less aggressive when the conciliator said to him: 'I expect you are feeling very angry with your wife for leaving you and the children and I can imagine how difficult it must be to think about meeting with her when you feel so angry. But these discussions are often more helpful than people expect them to be and I do hope you will decide to come.'

New partners and cohabitees

A parent who becomes involved with someone else, outside their marriage or established relationship, often keeps this secret because he or she feels guilty, confused and uncertain about the new relationship. The discovery of the extra-marital relationship may come as a devastating shock to an unsuspecting husband or wife, who may immediately petition for divorce without discussion or reflection. Alternatively, he or she may deny what has happened and refuse to take action of any kind, even pretending to the children that the other parent is working away from home. One mother, Mrs Evans, was unable to see that she might have contributed to the difficulties which led to her husband leaving home for someone else. She was a very religious woman and it was difficult to question her strong belief in the sanctity of marriage and her conviction that her husband would soon see the truth about 'that evil woman' (his new girlfriend). Mrs Evans was not willing to 'give' her husband a divorce, believing she must set the children a good example by maintaining that the marriage was not over as far as she was concerned.

A parent who raises moral objections to the children meeting the other parent's new partner or even learning of their existence may use this as a defence against the acute pain of recognising that their marriage is actually over. Sometimes the virtuous protestations of an apparently blameless partner are also used to punish the other parent by preventing their access to the children. Some parents are however genuinely worried that a person whom they regard as immoral or dangerously unreliable will harm the children or have a bad influence on them. These fears cannot necessarily be dealt with through rational discussion and in some cases they may be well founded and require investigation. If a parent seems to have serious cause for thinking that the children are at risk, he or she must be urged to contact an appropriate welfare agency and the conciliator must check that this has been followed through. But parents' objections are often based on moral concerns which may not affect the children as much as they imagine. Mitchell (1985) found that children often saw no difference between legal marriage and cohabitation: they were mainly concerned about how their parents got on with each other, where they would be living and who would be taking care of them.

In the case of Mrs Evans who was mentioned earlier, it was helpful to explore what she thought would happen that would harm or upset the children. One of her strongest objections to staying access was that the children might find their father in bed with his girlfriend. Mr Evans could see this would confuse them and he agreed to delay staying access for a while, until they had all had more time to settle down. He emphasised that when it did take place he would not make his sexual relationship with his girlfriend blatantly obvious to the children, but would introduce her as a good friend whom he hoped they would like too. This reassured Mrs Evans to some extent but did not remove her strong underlying fear of losing the children. She needed direct and repeated reassurance from her husband that he was not trying to take the children away from her and that his girlfriend was in no way a substitute or rival mother. After getting this reassurance from him, Mrs Evans agreed to the children going out with their father on his own, initially, and a family meeting was arranged so that these arrangements could be explained to the children.

Conciliators are sometimes taken aback by the unexpected appearance of a cohabitee or step-parent at a meeting intended only for the two natural parents. This is likely to cause great distress to the unsupported single parent. In the case of another couple, Mr and Mrs Mason, Mrs Mason's cohabitee, Mr Pritchard, turned up unexpectedly although the appointment letter had asked only Mr and Mrs Mason to come to the meeting as the children's parents, suggesting that another appointment could be arranged later for Mrs Mason and Mr Pritchard if they wished. Mr Pritchard's attempt to force his way into the meeting between the parents presented the conciliator with a difficult problem. She swallowed the impulse to get annoyed or flustered, greeting him in a friendly manner and saying how helpful it was of him to come. This took the wind out of his sails to some extent and he then agreed to some complicated boxing and coxing, in which the conciliator first saw Mr and Mrs Mason for half an hour to explain the help she was offering, then Mrs Mason was seen briefly with Mr Pritchard so that he was kept in the picture, and finally another three-quarters of an hour was spent with Mr and Mrs Mason. It was essential to have two separate waiting-areas so that this could be managed without Mr Pritchard and Mr Mason coming face to face before they were both ready to cope with the encounter. The use of two waiting areas is helpful in most cases, to avoid rows or hostile silence before conciliation begins.

Gathering relevant facts

A family therapist or counsellor may start by asking the family or individual client to explain the problem which has brought them. Conciliators, on the other hand, tend to avoid open-ended questions at the start, because this can result in one parent launching into an angry tirade which may be more than the other can tolerate. It is important for conciliators to take control initially, because this may be the only way of enabling some parents to stay in the same room and hear each other. Focused questions can establish who is living where, how long the couple has been apart, where the children are living and so on, checking information from a referral form if this is available. Some conciliators draw genograms (see James and Wilson, 1986, pp. 133–7) to help families see more clearly who belongs to the family and where each member fits in, but this needs to be done carefully to avoid causing distress or offence. The focus in conciliation needs to be on constructing a clearer picture, rather than offering therapeutic insights.

One parent's address may be strictly confidential but it is possible to establish how far apart they live, without giving addresses. Questions clarifying what is agreed or not agreed can be put in a friendly, informal style which helps people feel more comfortable. Basic points of agreement should be stressed, as well as identifying what is in dispute. It is helpful to comment on a major area of agreement, for example that the children should remain in familiar surroundings and attend the same schools, because parents have often forgotten that they agree about anything.

Weakland and colleagues (1974) advise against the use of questions beginning with 'why?' because they encourage blaming or defensive answers. This is particularly relevant in conciliation, where couples habitually blame each other for whatever has gone wrong between them. Brannen and Collard (1982) found in their study of marriage breakdown that there were no cases in which the partners accepted equal responsibility for what had gone wrong. There were several blaming patterns, of which the most common was a high-conflict pattern of mutual blaming in which accusations were flung backwards and forwards. Questions beginning 'when?' and 'how?' can reduce blaming, by helping parents give concrete examples of what is currently happening and what they want to achieve.

Conciliators vary in the extent to which they allow discussion about the past. Saposnek (1983) tells parents he will ask for background information only when he needs it and that he will stop them giving information he has not asked for, to prevent them getting sidetracked. Howard and Shepherd (1987), on the other hand, believe it is often necessary to work on unresolved issues from the past in order to help parents achieve an emotional divorce. The common denominator between these contrasting approaches is the control that conciliators need to exercise over the *process* of clarifying key issues. Precisely phrased questions can be used to pinpoint areas of agreement and disagreement and to reduce – or sometimes heighten – the emotional temperature of the discussion.

Containing and pre-empting conflict

Rules that parents may not interrupt or swear at each other help contain open conflict. But angry people may need to release at least some of their anger before they can begin to talk more rationally. The problem about this is that the anger easily takes over to such an extent that they become too distraught to continue the discussion. Often the anger has been bottled up for some time, so that when the couple meet face to face it erupts with alarming intensity. Conciliators may fear this elemental anger and try to stifle it with soothing words about agreements and co-operation, to no avail. Both parents may actually collude with each other in showing outsiders how bitterly they fight. A warring couple may thus jointly win the 'battle for initiative' (Whitaker, 1977) by showing conciliators that they are not strong enough to manage their conflict, thus fulfilling everyone's fears of escalating chaos.

One angry father who was demanding access to his four-year-old daughter constantly provoked his wife by making snide references to her boyfriend. She rose to these attacks just as he evidently expected and in this way the father scored points and prevented any useful discussion taking place. The conciliator took charge by saying to the father 'I'm sure you don't really think that Jim (wife's boyfriend) ought to be allowed to decide the contact between you and your daughter and therefore I'm going to insist in this meeting that Jim stays out of the room, as it were, so that you and Eva (wife) can just talk about Susie (their daughter)'. This intervention took the pressure off Eva and stopped her husband dominating the meeting, while acknowledging that decisions about Susie belonged to both parents. There was still a risk that if Jim, the boyfriend, felt excluded he might sabotage the access arrangements but as he did not feel Susie was his concern, this did not in fact happen. Where step-parents or new partners do share responsibility for the children, it is important to involve them in whatever way seems appropriate and accept-able to the parents. If both parents have new partners, a meeting with both couples together may be helpful, if they are all willing (see the case example in Chapter 6).

There are various ways of managing conflict so that it does not swamp sessions and prevent any useful work taking place. Conciliators need to use an approach which maximises their own personal qualities such as warmth, directness and, if appropriate, humour. Tension is sometimes reduced in unexpected ways. For example, one particularly stormy session came to a head when the wife made a dramatic exit, only to find she had walked into the broom cupboard by mistake. Even she was forced to laugh, and she then sat down and continued the discussion. Some spontaneity from con-ciliators is helpful and it is important to use plain, straight-forward language and to avoid legal and social work jargon.

Another way to pre-empt conflict, also recommended by Saposnek (1983), is to say to parents something on these lines: 'We are going to assume that the two of you hate each other and would much rather not be here at all. But we understand you have come to this meeting because you both care about your children and want them to be able to settle down. The problems are obviously not simple – or else you would have solved them already – and we are not expecting to solve them in just one discussion today. Usually we see parents two or three times. First we try to understand how you see your position and what the alternatives are, without either of you being under pressure to take decisions today which you might regret later.' It is most important to recognise and applaud the efforts parents make to do what they think will help their children, often at considerable personal cost. Recognising their hostile feelings towards each other may elicit a frosty acknowledgement that this is just how they feel, but sometimes it produces a smile and an assurance that things are not quite as bad as that. These responses help conciliators gauge the level of conflict and adjust their approach accordingly.

The need to disagree

When one parent declares, as they frequently do, 'the only way we are going to settle this is by going to court', it may be more effective to look at the likely time-scale and consequences of going to court than to try to coerce them into an agreement which may break down once they leave the room. Some information about the court's procedures may identify misconceptions about the legal process and the roles and powers of registrars, court welfare officers and judges. Neutral information can be given about legal procedures, the likely period for processing a legal aid application, the amount of time normally available at an in-court conciliation appointment and possible outcomes in court. Conciliators should advise parents not only to check these points with their solicitors but also to inquire how long the proceedings might take and whether they are liable to incur the Law Society's statutory charge if they are legally aided.

Information-giving can be a useful way of diverting parents from a particularly heated issue on which they have reached a deadlock. Divorcing couples are frequently ignorant of the legal process of divorce and a short factual input from a conciliator can emphasise aspects of the divorce process that are common to both parents. One mother said 'We need a judge with the wisdom of Solomon to decide who is right'. She had left her two young children with their father and they were squaring up for a bitter contest over the children and the home. However, this couple came to realise that even the wisest judges cannot produce perfect solutions and that parents know their own children better than a judge can ever do. This mother said 'I wouldn't be able to tell you that I think the children need their father more than me, if you were writing a report about us. But because this is private I can say how I really feel'. This couple had reversed roles during their marriage, with the father staying at home to look after the children. The mother finally decided that it was better for the children for this arrangement to continue, despite the loss it entailed for her. She was put in touch with Match (Mothers Apart From Their Children) and found them very helpful.

Re-framing

'To reframe means to change the conceptual and/or emotional setting or viewpoint in relation to which a situation is
experienced and to place it in another frame which fits the
"facts" of the same concrete situation equally well or even
better, and thereby changes its whole meaning' (Watzlawick,
Weakland and Fisch 1974, pp. 92–109). A positive reframing
of apparently negative behaviour or statements can help
change perceptions and validate positions. It is particularly
helpful in conciliation, where parents tend to read a hostile
intention into every word or gesture from each other. This
hostility may be only one facet of a complex interaction
between them and conciliators often need to reframe aggressive or defensive behaviour as having a positive and protective function for the family as a whole. Persistent wrangling
over times of access visits can be reframed as evidence of both
parents' commitment to the children and of a continuing
struggle to achieve the right balance for all concerned.

One rather depressed father complained that his former
wife was blocking his access to the children. She retorted that
he had no idea how to look after them. Her fierce protective-
ness was reframed by the conciliator as extreme conscien-
tiousness in looking after the children without help from
other people. The father had apparently spent little time with
the children before he left home and it was difficult for him to
argue that they were missing him. The conciliator praised the
mother for the good job she was doing and suggested that she
also owed it to herself to enjoy herself occasionally, without
feeling it was wrong to do so. The mother, who had looked
very tired and careworn when she arrived, responded to this
encouragement and in reply to some prompting from the
conciliator she began to tell the father how he ought to handle
each of the children. In sharing her picture of each child with
the father, she began to show faint confidence that he could
manage them for short periods. A trial visit was planned and
at a subsequent family meeting the children talked about
what they had done with their father and the parents looked
less depressed.

The emphasis in this chapter has been mainly on practical work with separated parents to help them plan for the future and reach joint decisions about their children. Conciliation and mediation are usually very brief forms of intervention and a carefully planned, systematic approach is needed to make as much progress as possible in a short time. The structure of discussions is all-important, but structure alone does not engage and hold distressed and angry people. Conciliators' warmth, sensitivity and genuine concern for each adult and child may help sustain them while they try to redefine and re-organise their relationships in old and new family systems.

6

Family Problems After Divorce

When conflict continues between parents after divorce, the parent who defines the cause of the problem often succeeds in deciding the remedy as well. Cause-and-effect explanations may justify a particular course of action but they are usually too limited to encompass the complexity of family relationships. Ending stressful access visits may appear to ease friction and let wounds heal, giving children and parents a chance to settle down. But this solution may meet the needs of adults rather than the needs of children and even the parent who wants a 'clean break' may find one set of problems has been exchanged for another. Broken links between family members affect the family as a whole, not only those who lose contact. A broken link may put more pressure on the remaining links, with the result that these suffer from overload and may burn out or fracture in their turn. Loss of contact with an absent father may draw children closer to their mother, but in some cases the relationship between the mother and one or more of the children becomes so strained that it eventually breaks down as well.

Children find it very difficult to cope with the pressures parents put on them when they persistently run each other down, either directly to the children or in their hearing (Rosen, 1977). Some children react by rejecting the parent they perceive as responsible for causing the breakup, others make secret visits to the absent parent behind the custodial parent's back, and even quite young children sometimes run away from home in search of a parent whom they have come to idealise in their imagination. The person they find may sadly fail to match this fantasy. When these children reach adulthood, a string of broken relationships may reflect a continuing search for the perfect parent they believe they once had.

Some rebellion against parental authority is a normal reaction in teenagers and part of their way of establishing their own identity and autonomy. Divorced parents may overreact to typical teenage behaviour, forgetting that they might have had the same problems even in a comparatively stable marriage. However, those who compete for their children's affections do not provide the safe boundaries of parental support and control that teenagers need in learning to rely on their own controls. Parents who disagree fundamentally on issues that cause arguments in many families, such as clothes, drinking, smoking and staying out late pull their children in opposite directions instead of encouraging negotiation and compromise. A rebellious teenager may be tempted to run from the more controlling parent to the one who seems more permissive, thus learning a negative pattern of escaping from authority whenever it becomes irksome. Parents who want to punish each other through the children may covertly incite them to be 'difficult', implying that the other parent's problems in managing them are solely of their own making. Linda, a 14-year-old who lived with her father and brother after her mother left home, rebelled against her father's discipline as a way of showing her anger with her parents. She manipulated both of them and each parent blamed the other for causing her problems. This usually ended in Linda storming away from both of them in furious protest. In conciliation the parents were helped to look at how these situations escalated and their mutual fear that Linda might run away from home motivated them to work together. Linda began to settle down when she found her mother supporting her father's decisions, instead of attacking them.

Access disputes are often a channel for continuing attachments between parents who cannot let go of each other emotionally. Most children are very sensitive to the strong emotional currents flowing between their parents and they are liable to become transmitters, picking up non-verbal signals as well as verbal ones and acting out the blocked or hostile messages they receive. The role of family transmitter is very stressful and children may show signs of emotional disturbance both before and after parental separation and divorce. James and Wilson (1984) found that 63 per cent of the families in their sample who were the subject of a divorce court welfare report said that one or more of their children were showing behavioural problems. Half the children were reported as having eating or sleeping difficulties, temper tantrums or other disturbed behaviour at home or at school, both before and after their parents' separation and nearly a third developed one or more of these problems after the separation. The incidence of behaviour problems was higher in families with three or more children.

The incomplete emotional divorce

Enmeshed couples (see Chapter 2) often seek to enlist welfare agencies to help them continue their fight rather than end it. One of the most bewildering and frustrating aspects of working with such couples is the depth of their ambivalence towards each other. They may be driven by simultaneous feelings of relief and loss, hatred and love, the need both to cling and to reject – and these contradictory impulses prevent cleancut solutions. Marital relationships do not disintegrate overnight and the feelings of being closely bound up with another person are not easily withdrawn and placed else-where. The theory of attachment, which focused originally on children's affectional bonds (Bowlby, 1969, 1973, 1980), applies to adult relationships as well, particularly to relation-ships between couples who have lived together as man and wife, whether legally married or not.

Kitson and colleagues (1983) identified four items which can be used to measure the strength of continuing attachment between divorced couples. These are: spending a lot of time thinking about the former partner; wondering what he or she is doing; doubting that the divorce has really happened; and feeling that it will never be possible to get over it. The researchers studied the varying adjustment to divorce among black and white couples from manual to upper-middle social classes in Cleveland, Ohio. Individuals were interviewed within six to ten months of filing for divorce and at this time about three quarters of them had been separated for less than a year. All but thirteen per cent expressed some sense of continuing attachment to their former partner and although these feelings generally faded over time, the majority still felt partly attached to each other at the time of the third follow-up interview – over four years after the physical separation. The presence of dependent children makes it much harder for parents to disengage fully from each other and the researchers found that painful feelings of attachment were often revived when parents had contact concerning their children. The sharp pain of seeing and then leaving each other again may explain why so many divorced parents try to avoid access visits or fail to manage them constructively. Social workers need to understand the long-standing nature of these deep emotional ties and the normality of ambivalent feelings which may be manifested in irrational push-and-pull behaviour. Divorce does not 'end everything': it alters family structure and living arrangements, but the dynamics which led to the divorce frequently persist afterwards and children may be entangled in family conflict long after the legal divorce has been finalised.

Brief intervention by conciliators or court welfare officers may have little impact on couples who are still so intensely bound up with each other that they would rather fight than experience the emptiness of total loss. Courts faced with these intractable disputes may make a matrimonial supervision order so that a social worker or probation officer can undertake further work with the family and keep the children's welfare under review.

Matrimonial supervision orders – a neglected area of social work practice

The number of supervision orders made in matrimonial and other family proceedings increased enormously in the sixties and seventies but since 1983 it has begun to fall again. The

Probation Statistics for 1985 show that 8840 children were subject to matrimonial supervision orders in that year, compared with 14 520 in 1982. The much smaller number of children subject to guardianship supervision has also dropped, while wardship figures show little change. One of the main reasons for the reduction is that orders are being discharged sooner, particularly those assigned to the probation service. Judges are now more inclined to make short-term orders, as recommended in the DHSS Review of Child Care Law (1985a) and by the Booth Committee (Report 1985). The Law Commission (1987) has proposed that the initial duration of supervision orders should be fixed for one year, unless otherwise ordered. Some courts have evolved a system in which short-term orders are assigned to the probation service where the problems seem to be mainly connected with parental conflict, while longer-term orders are assigned to social services where there are concerns about childcare. These criteria are being applied systematically in some areas, unlike the apocryphal case quoted by Griew and Bissett-Johnson (1975) in which magistrates on the domestic panel apparently said they were assigning a supervision order to probation rather than social services because the child in question needed discipline rather than love!

Matrimonial and other domestic supervision orders generally follow a recommendation from a court welfare officer. James and Wilson (1984) found little evidence, however, of consistency among probation officers when recommending supervision. In some cases where supervision was recommended, the children showed marked disturbance but in other cases involving similar problems no supervision order was called for. There also seems to be considerable uncertainty as to what constitutes good practice once an order has been made. Griew and Bissett-Johnson (1975) pointed out over ten years ago that there was little knowledge of social work practice in relation to matrimonial supervision orders and this neglect has not yet been adequately rectified (see however Wilkinson, 1981). The lack of debate about effective ways of exercising supervision may be largely due to the pressures of other statutory work. Hard pressed probation officers and social workers may be glad to have inactive supervision orders as a means of lightening their otherwise heavy case-loads. Some local authorities have internal pro-cedures specifying that contact must be made with each child under supervision at least once every three months. But there are no national guide-lines and some orders lie fallow without any regular check or review. Re-organisation and changes of staff can make it difficult to plan work and carry it through over a period of time and prolonged supervision undermines parents' confidence and responsibilities, as the Booth Com-mittee recognised (1985, para. 4.139).

Statutory powers in matrimonial supervision orders

Divorce courts and the magistrates' domestic courts can place a 'child of the family' or other minor under the supervision of a probation officer or local authority social worker if 'there are exceptional circumstances making it desirable that the child (or minor) shall be under the supervision of an independent person' (Guardianship of Minors Act 1971, Section 9(1)). The legislation provides no guidance to the courts as to what kind of circumstances should be regarded as sufficiently exceptional to warrant the making of an order. In the absence of any national guide-lines, there is wide vari-ation between different judges and different courts: Ports-mouth made 76 orders in 1985 whereas Newcastle made none at all (Priest and Whybrow, 1986, para 7.20). One of the most striking features of the legislation is that it confers virtually no powers on supervising officers. They have no power to insist on seeing the child who is the subject of the order, either with a parent or alone, nor to see either parent nor gain access to the home. They cannot require parents to inform them of changes of family address, though a requirement that such a change be notified is sometimes included in the order. The supervisor's only explicit power is to apply to the court for the order to be varied or discharged and even this power varies according to the court in which the order was made. The supervisor may apply in the divorce court for an order committing the child to the care of the local authority but may not do so in the magistrates' court. The supervisor can ask the divorce court, but not the magistrates' court, for 'directions as to the exercise of his powers', but as nobody seems to know what they are, this is not likely to be helpful (Hoggett, 1981). The Law Commission (1986) has proposed that the same requirements could be attached to supervision orders as to orders made in care proceedings, addressed to either parent or to the child.

The purpose of matrimonial supervision orders

The social worker or probation officer to whom a supervision order is allocated may not be present in court when the order is made and judges do not always state its purpose, although this is recommended (Booth Report 1985, para. 4.140). Sometimes the social services department may not even be aware of the existence of the order, owing to administrative delays or the non-appearance of a copy of the court order. The court is not required to consult the social services department before making the order and judges may be anxious not to direct trained social workers how to exercise their professional skills. However, it is very difficult for social workers to introduce themselves to families if they do not understand why the supervision order was made and the term 'supervision' has unfortunate associations with deviant or criminal behaviour. Matrimonial supervision orders are inappropriately named. Placing a child under supervision implies that the problems lie with the child, whereas work usually needs to be undertaken with the parents and not only with the child who is named in the order. Renaming them 'family supervision orders' might be better. Both parents should be encouraged to come to court so that the reasons for the order can be explained and their co-operation enlisted, as far as possible.

The limited information generally provided on matrimonial supervision orders suggests that they tend to be ordered where there is continuing conflict between the parents or because of concerns about conditions in the home and/or standards of childcare. Rather surprisingly, Priest and Whybrow (1986) found that over 50 per cent of supervision orders were made in conjunction with joint custody orders. This was particularly noticeable in courts in the south of England with higher than average rates of joint custody orders (Exeter, Guildford and Wandsworth), suggesting that supervision orders are used to support the concept of joint custody and resolve ongoing difficulties between the parents. These orders point to the need for carefully planned conflict management work with both parents and the children, rather than occasional supportive visits to the custodial parent and the children.

Whom do supervising officers see as their client?

Griew and Bissett-Johnson (1975) found that the quality and appropriateness of work carried out under matrimonial supervision orders was fairly haphazard. They seem to attract amazingly little attention either from fieldworkers or their managers, despite the large numbers of children who remain under supervision for long periods of time. Aware of what seemed like a black hole in social work practice and literature, two colleagues and I undertook a very small study during 1984–5 of social work practice under matrimonial supervision orders, with the co-operation of Avon Probation Service and Avon Social Services Department. This study, which was not necessarily representative of work throughout the county, showed that most supervisors identified the mother or the mother-and-children as the main focus of their work. Occasionally a father living alone was the identified client and in a few cases the grandparents who were looking after the children. None of the social workers or probation officers who took part in this project seemed to see the whole family – natural parents, step-parents, children, grandparents – as the focus of their work. In nearly all the families, one or both parents had remarried or were cohabiting with a new partner but supervisors usually selected one particular sub-system in what Ahrons (1980) termed the 'binuclear' family and worked exclusively with this sub-system. In over a third of the cases, no attempt had been made to see the children's father although his whereabouts were known: his willingness to be involved and potential co-operation were untested. Joint meetings with both parents had rarely been contemplated. Workers were encouraged in the course of the project to consider the possible benefits of arranging a meeting with both parents or the whole family, involving a co-worker where this was likely to be helpful. One of the difficulties is that a worker who is perceived as helping one parent, usually the custodial parent, may be seen by the other parent as 'taking sides'. If possible, the worker should try to maintain a non-partisan position but this is not always possible or appropriate. Some parents need a great deal of personal support and if the worker is primarily supporting one parent, it may help to involve a co-worker at a particular meeting so that the other parent feels adequately supported as well.

Brief work under a matrimonial supervision order

The indefinite duration of many matrimonial supervision orders tends to foster apathy and defeatist attitudes in families and social workers alike. It is easy to feel that the problems are insoluble if the court expects the order to remain in force until the child reaches 18. Now, with the increasing use of short-term orders and growing experience of conciliation, mediation and other conflict management techniques, more brief work is being done under these orders, with encouraging results. When the problems stem mainly from continuing parental conflict rather than long-term concerns about standards of childcare, supervisors, like welfare officers, may decide to arrange a family meeting to clarify current difficulties and discuss with the family how the problems might be eased. In the following case, drawn from the Avon project on matrimonial supervision, a proactive attempt was made to involve both parents in a joint meeting, despite a long history of conflict between them.

Case study 1 – the Thomas family

Matrimonial supervision orders had been made in the divorce court in respect of Cheryl and Suzanne Thomas, now aged nine and six. Both parents had remarried in the two years since their divorce and Mr Thomas' access to the girls was strongly opposed by their mother. Briefly, the problems confronting the supervising officer may be summarised as follows:

(a) The parents' inability to have any constructive communication with each other. Messages between the two households were usually sent verbally via Cheryl or in a note written by Mr Thomas' new wife. The parents refused to meet each other and as they lived fifty miles apart the geographical distance posed a further problem. From the supervisor's point of view, it was much easier to visit the mother and children and support the new stepfamily, leaving Mr Thomas to make frustrated and furious telephone calls each time access visits went awry.

(b) Each parent's intense dislike and suspicion of the other's new partner. They tended to project their unresolved anger on to the new partners, thus easing the uncomfortable ambivalence in their feelings towards each other. Both parents complained constantly to the children about the other step-parent and made it clear that they were not to be trusted in any way. The new partners had considerable influence in their own household and any work with the natural parents had to take this influence into account.

(c) Suzanne's hysterical reactions when she caught sight of her father. She would scream uncontrollably, thus acting as an alarm signal for both families that contact between the former marital partners was dangerous and frightening. The supervising officer was uncertain whether to encourage Mr Thomas to give up trying to see Suzanne, who had grown close to her stepfather and called him 'Daddy'. She was also unsure whether she could help Suzanne by seeing her on her own or possibly with Cheryl.

(d) The depressing prospect for the supervisor of acting indefinitely as a go-between, carrying complaints backwards and forwards without relieving anyone's distress. This raised the question of whether the time and effort that the Thomas family could easily absorb would be better spent with other families with less intractable problems.

Grasping courage in both hands, the supervisor decided to ask both parents to help her review the current situation at a joint meeting in her office, at which one of her colleagues would be present to give additional help. Two attempts to convene a meeting failed because Mr Thomas cancelled, saying his wife was ill. The supervisor persevered and although Mr Thomas did not reply to her third letter, he appeared at the appointed time with his new wife, while the children's mother (now Mrs West) arrived with her new husband. The supervisor had not expected both step-parents but quickly negotiated that she and her co-worker would spend an hour with the natural parents and then, if everyone was willing, a further hour with both couples. This was accepted, and a painful hour was spent going over unfinished business between the two parents. Some of the matters they raised could have seemed trivial but were actually significant symbolic issues, such as the fact that one of them had walked out of court without saying anything to the other. The mother complained that Mr Thomas' letters or postcards to the girls were written by his new wife, Julie, and he explained that he felt embarrassed at the girls seeing his poor handwriting and spelling. When the first hour was up, both parents and the two workers had a much-needed coffee break and were joined by the two step-parents for a further hour.

By this time, some of the bottled up grievances had been released and discussions in the second hour moved into positive problem-solving. The parents had imagined each other's new partner as larger than life bogey figures and they were surprised to discover that they were ordinary, pleasant people who got on well with each other! Julie, the second wife, who had been seen by the Wests as 'that awful woman' turned out to be a rather shy girl of 25 who was not sure how to handle the children. When the letter issue was raised, Mr Thomas agreed to copy out letters written for him by Julie so that the girls would feel he had taken the trouble to write himself. He also undertook not to take them to the pub, as he had done on one occasion. Mr West, who had previously refused to let Mr Thomas into the house, suggested that the best way to deal with Suzanne's distress was for Mr Thomas to come down once a month and chat or play with her for a while in their home, without pressure to go out with him. If she seemed happy to go out with him and Cheryl, this could happen without any fuss. At the end of the second hour, a number of specific agreements were summarised and the supervisor undertook to send a copy of the summary to both couples, with the mutually agreed objective that if all went according to plan she would apply to the court a few months later to have the supervision order discharged.

The positive outcome in the above case could not have been predicted with any certainty from the previous long history of conflict. The new partners who had been blamed as the main 'cause' of the trouble proved to be effective mediators who made helpful suggestions and eased the tensions between the parents.

Psychological parenting after divorce

A divorced parent bringing up children alone or with a new partner may strongly resist the other parent having continuing contact with the children, especially if he (or she) had very little to do with them prior to the separation. It is often assumed that to be a parent, one must have physical care of the children and some social workers as well as some parents seem to see physical and psychological parenting as inseparable. Empirical research on children in care (Holman, 1973; Thorpe, 1980) is relevant here, since the findings show the extent to which children retain a concept of having two parents, even if they do not live with them and have little contact. Most young children can form and sustain relationships with the important adults in their lives and they can generally tolerate short periods of physical separation, provided they do not feel abandoned psychologically. Thorpe (1980) found in her study of children in long-term fostercare that children who maintained even tenuous contact with their natural parents felt less rejected and were better able to settle in their foster-home. They did not suffer conflicts of loyalty and even occasional access to their natural parents helped bolster their self-esteem and sense of identity.

The importance of maintaining contact with both parents is well recognised by social workers in the context of separation and divorce but it seems to receive low priority once children are received into care. Gibson and Parsloe (1984) found many social workers believed that children need exclusive parenting *either* in a nuclear family *or* in a substitute family. As a result, parents were often prevented or discouraged from visiting their children in care, despite the declared policy in social services departments to restore children to their parents as soon as possible. Research carried out by Rowe and Lambert (1973) showed that of 7000 children in the long-term care of local authorities or voluntary organisations, 5000 required a secure legal relationship short of adoption which did not entirely sever their links with their natural parents. Although continuing contact with parents is one of the strongest factors predicting the child's return home, many children in foster or residential care have no contact with either of their parents (Millham, Bullock, Hosie and Gower, 1985). Millham and colleagues found that nearly three-quarters of the 450 children in their study had great difficulty maintaining contact with their parents and that the import-ance of these links was not given sufficient priority by social workers.

Social workers' knowledge of child development needs to be applied consistently, so that the same principles are followed in working with intact families, separated, divorced and stepfamilies and adoptive and fosterfamilies. Wherever possible, children need to know their parents still care about them and have not rejected them, even if it is not possible for them to live together. Similarly, parents and parent-substitutes need reassurance that it is possible for children to maintain beneficial attachments to several key adults and more than one environment, without having to choose between them. Grief and anger may be long-lasting, but family processes in the present are powerful conditioners of adjustment to the past. Social work intervention may therefore be more effective if workers focus on current communications and interaction in families, rather than on one child or parent's reactions to the past.

Some common problems in stepfamilies

Post-divorce family conflict is often increased by myths and fantasies which can be dispelled only through face-to-face meetings and direct dialogue. Fantasies about step-parents are very powerful and as Visher and Visher (1985) pointed out, the features that distinguish stepfamilies from biological families have gone largely unnoticed until recently. Stepfamilies are by no means a homogeneous group: they include many variations of family structure which may call for different kinds of adjustment or reorganisation (Robinson, 1980; Burgoyne and Clark, 1982). Remarried couples often struggle hard to be the same as 'ordinary' families, trying to banish ghosts from the past who remind them that they are a stepfamily. The other natural parent may refuse to be obliterated, however, and professionals who become involved may strive to maintain the children's contact with this parent. Maddox (1980) and Hodder (1985) draw from their own first-hand experience in describing the pressures on step-parents to act the part of instant parent without having any script for their role or any clear mandate to discipline as well as care for their stepchildren. Children may deeply resent a newcomer who has apparently caused the breakup of their parents' marriage. They may fear being displaced in the remaining parent's affections and may desperately need reassurance and extra attention just when the new couple are in the honeymoon phase of their relationship.

Ferri's (1984) longitudinal study of children in stepfamilies, based on data collected for the National Child Development Study, showed that poor relationships between children and step-parents were much more common when the original family had been broken by divorce than when a natural parent had died. Unfortunately this study did not seek specific information about the children's contact with their absent parent and it was often unclear whether they were describing their feelings about their stepfather or biological father. The ambiguity in the way questions were phrased underlines Ferri's own observation that 'the confusion surrounding the roles of step-parents and non-custodial natural parents is part of the wider normative vacuum in our society which results from its failure to come to terms with the consequences of high rates of divorce and remarriage' (p. 105).

Longitudinal studies show that the risk of breakdown in families with a stepfather is very high. In Ferri's study, one in five of the children who lived with a stepfather at 11 was no longer in this situation at 16. This is not to deny that many stepfamilies are stable and that many children become strongly attached to their step-parent. A substantial minority of these children are however very unhappy and insecure and some become seriously disturbed. It may not be reasonable to expect parents to deny their own emotional needs in deciding whether or not to remarry, but the way a new cohabitee or step-parent is introduced to the children is very important. More public education is needed to help parents with this difficult task: if children are given adequate explanation, support and reassurance, they are more likely to accept and cope with this further change in their lives.

Sager and colleagues (1983) found that conflict in stepfamilies was not only caused by the intrusion of unresolved problems from the past: tensions also arose because the members of the stepfamily were out of phase with each other's position in the family life-cycle. Step-parents who have not had children before may be thrown into difficult scenes with adolescent stepchildren, without having grown up with them as babies and toddlers. Others may bring young children from a previous relationship, compelling their partner to move backwards to an earlier stage of the family life-cycle which they thought they had left behind. Helping members become more aware of these tensions between different stages of the life-cycle may ease some of their anger and frustration towards each other.

Case study 2 – the Walker family

In a case referred to a conciliation service, a thrice-married husband, Joe Walker, was being asked by his first wife to agree to Mandy, their teenage daughter, moving to live with her. A number of adults would be affected by this change and the conciliator asked both parents who they thought should be consulted. This led to a meeting involving the father, his first wife, his third wife (but not the second one, as she was in America), the 20-year-old daughter of the first marriage and Mandy herself. Interestingly, all the women in the room seemed in agreement with each other and all of them seemed anxious not to confront Joe, who apparently had a fierce temper. The third wife and older daughter acted as mediators between Joe and Mandy's mother, who had not met for a long time. Joe stipulated first, that no solicitors would be involved and secondly, that the change of custody must be 'legal' although he was not prepared to attend a court hearing. The family, including Mandy herself, all agreed that it would be better for her to live with her mother and the conciliator then explained how they could apply to the court for a variation of the custody order, without incurring legal costs as Joe was willing to countersign the application by Mandy's mother. The conciliator took care to involve Mandy's stepmother in this decision and seek her opinions, as she had been looking after Mandy and it was important that her role was acknowledged and valued.

Parents themselves often recognise that arrangements made when they separated or divorced need to be changed, because family circumstances have changed and/or the children's needs have changed. At different stages of their development, children may need more contact with one parent than another and it is very reassuring for them if a move or adjustment can be agreed without forcing them to reject one parent in favour of the other. This is a further reason for involving both parents in decision-making at the time of their divorce, as joint discussion at this critical point may set a pattern for the future and make it easier for them to renegotiate arrangements later on, if need be. Otherwise, a child who badly needs to move to the other parent may be left with the burden of making the move alone, or concealing his or her distress. Both these alternatives put a great deal of pressure on children. If their misery and confusion are not understood, a step-parent is liable to catch the full brunt of the child's anger and distress, causing the step-parent a great deal of anguish and guilt and putting the new marriage at risk. Step-parents and natural parents need to know that it is not a sign of failure to ask for help and that it is normal for families to experience some difficulties in making the transition from one family structure to another.

Support for stepfamilies

Until recently, little help has been available specifically for stepfamilies but in 1983 a new voluntary organisation, the National Stepfamily Association (Stepfamily), was formed in response to the evident need. Since then, the association has been almost overwhelmed by the flood of inquiries and requests for help. Its founder member and first general secretary, Elizabeth Hodder, reported at Stepfamily's second AGM in June 1986 that some 10 000 enquiries had been dealt with. Step-parents who have experienced similar problems can give new step-parents a great deal of support and guidance and there are a growing number of stepfamily support groups around the country, with professional consultants providing back-up. This partnership between professionals and community self-help groups supplements scarce professional resources, offering long-term support to families under stress and almost constant availability in ways that are acceptable to parents themselves.

7
Family Courts and Social Work Services

Conciliation services and court-related work with families need to be planned as part of a co-ordinated programme of family law reform. Otherwise, a puny conciliation effort may operate on the fringe of a powerful adversarial system without changing the way most families go through the legal process. The case for a family court has been argued so often (Finer Report, 1974; BASW, 1985; Law Society, 1986) that the arguments need not be repeated here. This chapter concentrates therefore on the role of social work services in a future family court and on the training, supervision and support which are particularly important in this stressful field of work.

The Family Courts Campaign

Many social workers are involved in the campaign for a unified family court to replace the present fragmented system in which three jurisdictions, High Court, County Courts and magistrates' courts, overlap with each other in matrimonial and family proceedings. Table 7.1 gives some indication of the volume of court proceedings affecting children in divorce and other civil cases. It is very difficult, however, to compile accurate and comprehensive statistics from the figures available. Custody and access orders are generally made in respect of more than one child in a family, so the number of children involved greatly exceeds the number of orders made. Some parents do not go to court at all and Table 7.1 may therefore

Table 7.1 *Court proceedings affecting children*

	High Court and County Courts	Magistrates' Courts
1. Decrees absolute of divorce 1985[1]	160 300	
2. Custody and access orders, High Court and county courts 1985[2]	90 000	
3. Custody and access orders, domestic courts, 1985[3]		20 000
4. Applications for maintenance orders or variations, 1984[4]	93 000	88 000
5. Applications for enforcement of maintenance, 1984[5]	3 000	104 000
6. Applications for personal protection orders, 1984[6]	22 000	11 000
7. Children made subject to local authority supervision, 1984/5 (matrimonial and family proceedings)[7]	←2 760 →	
8. Children made subject to supervision by the probation service, 1985 (matrimonial and family proceedings)[8]	←2 000 →	
9. Orders confirming wardship 1985[9]	2 252	
10. Adoption orders 1984[10]	7 500	1 100
11. Children admitted to care 1983/4 a) under the MCA 1973[11] and b) under the Family Law Reform Act 1969	a) 350 b) 238	
12. Children admitted to care in domestic court proceedings 1983/4[12]		120
13. Access orders to grandparents[13] 1984/5	21	100

NOTES:
1. Office of Population Censuses and Surveys, Divorces in England and Wales 1985. (OPCS 1986b).
2. Law Commission (1986) *Review of Child Custody Law* (Working Paper No. 96) p. 84, note 1.
3. see 2 above.
4. Interdepartmental Review of Family and Domestic Jurisdiction (1986) p. 16.
5. see 4 above.
6. see 4 above.
7. Law Commission (1987) Working Paper No. 100: *Care, Supervision and Interim Orders in Custody Proceedings*.
8. Probation Statistics 1985.
9. Judicial Statistics 1985, Table 4.2.
10. OPCS Survey (1986a) *Adoptions in England and Wales, 1984*.
11. DHSS (1986) *Report on Children in Care in England and Wales*, March 1984, Table A3.
12. see 12 above.
13. see 2 above, p. 164, note 93.

substantially underestimate the total numbers of children affected by family break-up. On the other hand, about a third of custody orders made in the divorce courts involve a pre-existing order made in the magistrates' domestic court (Priest and Whybrow, 1986, para. 3.9). This duplication of orders shows that many families go through more than one set of civil court proceedings. At the time of writing, there are no figures available yet on custodianship.

As the table indicates, there is a great deal of overlap between courts which have different powers to deal with essentially similar family problems. Appeals from the magistrates' courts go to the High Court or Crown Court, not the County Court.

A single example must suffice to show how decisions about a particular child can get entangled in several different jurisdictions. This case (J *v.* Devon County Council (Wardship: Jurisdiction) see *Family Law* (1986), vol. 16, p. 162) involved a boy aged seven who was in voluntary care and placed with foster-parents. His parents subsequently divorced and the divorce court made a matrimonial care order under section 43 of the Matrimonial Causes Act 1973. His mother appealed against the care order and when her appeal failed in the county court, she made a fresh application to the High Court under wardship proceedings. The local authority applied unsuccessfully to have the wardship application discharged and meanwhile the foster-parents started adoption proceedings in a different county court from the one which had granted the divorce and made the care order.

Twelve years ago, the Finer Committee deplored the 'great disorder caused by the patchwork nature of the present arrangements' (Report 1974, para. 4.342) but successive governments have shelved Finer's proposals, ostensibly on cost grounds. Hopes of action were revived in November 1983 when the Lord Chancellor announced a fresh inquiry into the feasibility and cost of a unified family court (*Hansard*, HL 21 November 1983). However, Lord Hailsham also expressed scepticism that such a court would 'usher in the millenium in the way that some of its supporters seem to suppose' (p. 36). Two and a half years later, the Lord

Chancellor's Department published its long-awaited paper on family courts, the Interdepartmental Review of Family and Domestic Jurisdiction (May 1986), which sets out the alternatives for the possible structure and organisation of a family court without making any commitment to further action. The Review's passive approach was criticised by the Family Courts Campaign, an energetic body which is snapping at central government heels and rounding up support for the family court from over a hundred statutory and voluntary organisations. Set up by the Association of County Councils in November 1985, the Family Courts Campaign has established that there is broad consensus not only on the concept of a family court but also on the way it should operate in practice. In its response to the Interdepartmental Review, entitled 'A Court Fit for Families', the Family Courts Campaign (1986) takes the view that a family court system is more than a judicial forum. 'It is the heart of a network of agencies and services available to families in trouble. The court itself therefore has responsibilities which are wider than judicial and would need to monitor those services on a continuous basis as a guarantee of service quality for service users' (para. 5.21).

Social work services in the family court

The experience of family courts in operation in Australia, New Zealand, Canada and the United States points to the importance of specialist court welfare and conciliation services which are directly accessible to the community as well as to the court itself. The first point of contact between individuals and the court may be the optimum time to refer them for crisis-orientated counselling and conciliation, since informal discussions at this stage may be more helpful to many families than formal court hearings. If parents are able to reach agreed decisions, the arrangements they work out for themselves can be endorsed by court orders made with mutual consent. Cases in which a court order is needed urgently can be referred for conciliation as well as being listed for a court hearing and by the time the hearing takes place, some problems may have been eased or at least clarified through conciliation. If no agreement is possible or where there is particular concern about the welfare of a child, the court would normally call for an inquiry and evaluation by a court counsellor who makes assessments for the court as well as seeking to help the family.

A family court intake service can respond to inquiries and pre-court referrals as well as taking formal referrals from the court itself. Inquirers can be given information about community-based services as well as information about the family court, to help them decide what kind of help or action is most appropriate to their particular difficulty. The Family Court of Jamaica has intake counsellors who are qualified and experienced social workers. They listen to people who call in person, clarify and assess their problems and refer them to non-legal as well as legal services. 'This approach has been so successful that at its inception the Court had difficulty coping with the number of people who came for assistance and there has been no reduction in the flood since' (Interdepartmental Review 1986, Appendix 3, para. 35).

In the Family Court of New Zealand, a counselling co-ordinator is attached to each registry to provide information, advice and brief crisis counselling. People can be referred by the counselling co-ordinator for up to six hours' free counselling or conciliation from a community-based service, but if this offer is not taken up and there is continuing dispute, the court has power to order a mediation conference chaired by a specialist Family Court judge. The atmosphere in these mediation conferences is kept as informal as possible. The judge does not act in a judicial capacity but has the power to make consent orders where agreements are reached. Most contested cases are settled informally either at the pre-court stage or at a mediation conference, leaving only a very small number to go to a full judicial hearing. Out of 4818 applications for custody orders in 1984, only 357 required a judicial decision (Priestley, 1984; New Zealand Department of Justice Statistics, 1984). The Family Court of New Zealand thus provides a flexible, three-stage response to the wide spectrum of problems that individuals and families bring to the court: (i) pre-court counselling and conciliation; (ii) court-ordered mediation conferences and (iii) judicial hearings.

Pioneer family court schemes in Canada show a very similar approach to the one being developed in New Zealand. The Frontenac Family Referral Service at Kingston, Ontario provides advisory and mediation services in the court precincts but not under the court's control: the service is run by an interdisciplinary committee of social work, mental health and legal professionals and by representatives of the local community. Since 1978, the service has been funded by the provincial government of Ontario. The diagram on page 142 shows that 40 per cent of referrals to the service are pre-court referrals made directly by one or both parties or by social work departments, compared with 60 per cent referred by the court. It has been estimated (Frontenac Report, 1984) that approximately 1500 children, half of them under the age of five, are involved each year in cases referred to the service and follow-up research suggests that the timing of the referral is extremely important. In a study of 81 cases involving at least one dispute per case, the settlement rate where mediation took place at the pre-court stage was 71 per cent, compared with a settlement rate of 54 per cent where mediation took place after court proceedings had started (Frontenac Report, 1984 p. 49). The main aim of the Frontenac scheme is to provide a front-line service to applicants and their families rather than a back-up service for judges, and as a result the number of cases requiring a full welfare investigation is relatively small.

It is significant that family court referral services in Canada and New Zealand use social work skills in intake assessment and crisis counselling, whereas applications to civil courts in England and Wales are usually made on paper and handled administratively by court clerks and clerical assistants. The creation of a new family court offers an opportunity to establish an intake and assessment service staffed by court counsellors on a rota basis, to help people at the critical point when they look for legal solutions to personal and family problems. Without such a service, the much-championed family court could easily become another bureaucratic institution, remote from the families it is supposed to help.

142

Figure 7.1 *Couples in crisis*

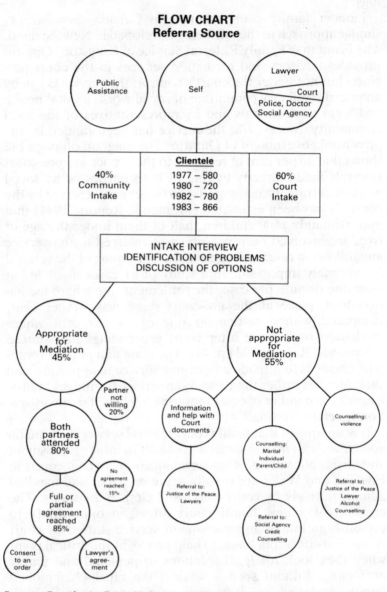

FLOW CHART
Referral Source

Public Assistance

Self

Lawyer
Court
Police, Doctor
Social Agency

Clientele

40% Community Intake	1977 – 580 1980 – 720 1982 – 780 1983 – 866	60% Court Intake

INTAKE INTERVIEW
IDENTIFICATION OF PROBLEMS
DISCUSSION OF OPTIONS

Appropriate for Mediation 45%

Partner not willing 20%

Both partners attended 80%

No agreement reached 15%

Full or partial agreement reached 85%

Consent to an order

Lawyer's agreement

Not appropriate for Mediation 55%

Information and help with Court documents

Referral to: Justice of the Peace Lawyers

Counselling: Marital Individual Parent/Child

Referral to: Social Agency Credit Counselling

Counselling: violence

Referral to: Justice of the Peace Lawyer Alcohol Counselling

Source: Couples in Crisis II, Frontenac Family Referral Service, Kingston, Ontario, Canada, 1984.

Children's panels and reporters in Scotland

As well as looking at models of the family court overseas, it is worth taking a careful look at the Scottish experience of children's panels in the juvenile justice system. Parents and children attend round-the-table meetings with a panel of lay people and professionals, who decide in consultation with the family what course of action should be taken. These meetings are convened by a Children's Reporter, who may be a lawyer or a social worker. The Reporter is responsible first of all for deciding whether a meeting is appropriate and then for recording the panel's decisions and making sure that everyone understands what steps are going to be taken in each case.

There are at least two valuable lessons to be learnt from this system which could be applied in future family courts in England and Wales. As Martin and Murray (1984) emphasise, even where a formal decision has to be taken, backed by the authority of a court, there are strong reasons for encouraging the direct participation of families in the decision-making process. 'Panel members are enabled to see family problems with a clarity and sense of perspective that formal reports alone cannot provide . . . and there is the further advantage that through the exchange of views parents may come to share in and identify with the eventual decision, thereby creating a basis for constructive work in any subsequent period of supervision' (p. 8). Inviting parents to contribute directly to professional debate and decisions about their children is not a new idea. Bell (1973) pointed out that participation became something of a 'hurrah word' in social policy in the sixties, when attempts were made to lower the barriers between the providers and receivers of social services. But much depends on how the theory of participation is put into practice. It can be a cover for paternalistic forms of social control, operated without the safeguards and accountability that formal justice provides (King, 1981; Freeman, 1984).

One of the most difficult aspects of attempts to involve parents in formal decisions about their children is the imbalance of power between families and the court. However hard professionals try to give power back to parents so that they retain responsibility for their own decisions, the parents may feel they have been railroaded into concessions which reflect professional preferences or values, rather than their own. Well-intentioned efforts may fail to achieve a genuine dialogue between anxious and possibly inarticulate individuals confronted by professionals who may have massive advantages in terms of personal authority, social prestige and verbal skills. 'It is temptingly easy for steps to involve parents to degenerate into more or less cynical manipulation, designed to bring about an ill-considered acceptance of panel decisions in which the family members have had no real part' (Martin and Murray 1984, p. 8). If we are to avoid what Freeman (1984) refers to as 'rampant interventionism', interfering in families while claiming to help them or their children, higher priority needs to be given to monitoring the work that is done and improving its quality. The DHSS Report on Social Work Decisions in Child Care (1985b) found a serious gulf between the values and expectations of social workers and their clients, a gulf which was often increased by problems of communication.

Family conferences and network meetings

Modern systems of electronic communication are becoming more sophisticated almost by the minute, whereas skills in person-to-person communication and negotiation are neglected and undervalued. Training in family dynamics and communication skills are needed not only to improve social work services to families but also to help social workers communicate with each other and with other professionals in carrying out related tasks and responsibilities. Social workers and probation officers are involved in formal and informal networks of social care and control and are therefore well-placed to identify and convene these intersecting networks. This calls for skills in network meetings and groupwork as well as in individual and conjoint work.

The conductor of an orchestra does not conduct duets between two individual voices or instruments – he tries to find and maintain the right balance between woodwind, strings, brass and percussion. Network meetings that bring together family members and professionals from different agencies are rather like an orchestra. The leaders of the network meeting need to manage it in a way that enables each contribution to be heard in an organised way, without allowing flutes and clarinets to be drowned by sounding brass or deafening percussion. Bentovim and Gilmour (1981) described their practice in difficult custody and access cases of convening all those who have 'living together' relationships, 'responsibility and authority' relationships and 'access relationships' – parents, children, social workers and possibly solicitors, plus other family members involved in decisions about the children – step-parents, foster and/or adoptive parents, grandparents. They stress the importance of maintaining a neutral position and avoiding alliances with any individual or subsystem.

Network meetings may help unlock particularly complex and stuck situations in which many people have become involved. If key people are brought together in the same place at the same time, they may gain better understanding of each other's perspective and degree of responsibility for decisions, and this increased understanding may produce better decisions and greater commitment to make them work. Dimmock and Dungworth (1985) emphasise that in statutory child care cases, the relationship between the social services department and the child who is the primary client can be the lever which produces change in a much larger system. Working outwards from this focal point, the network of significant adults can be defined and convened and the statutory powers conferred by the court can become 'the focus for bringing about sufficient intensity for change to take place' (p. 60). Dimmock and Dungworth emphasise the importance of structuring these meetings so that they are not simply ad hoc encounters or collisions between disconnected individuals. They distinguish network meetings from family therapy meetings and recommend that contributions should be invited from those present in a graded sequence which reflects relative degrees of responsibility in relation to the child who is the focus of concern. For example, a biological parent would be consulted before a step-parent but the step-parent's views would be sought and acknowledged.

In childcare cases, conciliation methods could be used to resolve disputes between the local authority and the child's natural parents, adoptive and/or foster-parents. If the local authority is seen as a 'parent' whose concerns for the child clash with those of the other parent(s) involved, a neutrally placed conciliator may be needed who is not aligned with any of these parental systems. Many cases could be referred for this kind of network conciliation, which could be provided by family court conciliators. If a formal court hearing is necessary, it need not be conducted on adversarial lines: it could take the form of a court-ordered conference conducted like a children's panel or network meeting, involving families and social workers but making it clear that if no satisfactory solution is reached, the final decision rests with the court. Family court conciliators could convene these conferences, on the basis that they would be non-partisan and have specialist skills to ease communication between families, other agencies and the court. This brings us to the question of how such a service could be organised and staffed.

A new family court welfare service

BASW's paper on Family Courts (November 1985) favours a new court welfare service that would be independent of the probation service and of local authority social service departments. This independence is vital, since the local authority may be a party to the proceedings in childcare cases. A new family court service could be staffed by qualified social workers with several years' experience of working with families and children in a statutory or voluntary agency. It would be two-pronged, undertaking welfare inquiries and conciliation as separate and distinct tasks. The National Association of Probation Officers takes a different view (NAPO, November 1985) arguing that as the probation service has extensive experience of providing welfare services to civil courts, it is the most appropriate agency to provide a welfare service to the new family court. Court welfare officers are acquiring considerable experience of conciliation and mediation and by 1985, two-thirds of the probation regions in England and Wales are running or helping to run some kind of conciliation service. Many probation officers believe a separate civil division of the probation service should be established with responsibility for court welfare work and conciliation and with a separate budget, though there is some concern that this might syphon off valuable expertise which is needed by the service as a whole.

The Family Courts Campaign (1986), to which BASW, NAPO and the Association of Chief Officers of Probation are affiliated, has declared a preference for a new, independent service which would absorb the functions of court welfare officers, conciliators, guardians *ad litem* and the Official Solicitor. Rather than calling this comprehensive service the Family Court Welfare Service, as the Family Courts Campaign proposes, it might be better entitled the Family Court Referral Service, since it should have an intake function and undertake conciliation and welfare inquiries as separate functions. The service could be independent in two respects. Firstly, it would not be able to act on behalf of any party to the proceedings, including the local authority. Secondly, instead of being run by the court or the Probation Service, it could be managed by a joint management committee representing local professions, community representatives and court staff. Conciliators and welfare officers appointed to this service would need to be carefully selected and adequate resources should be made available for their training, support and supervision.

Training for court welfare work and conciliation

The pressure to extend court welfare work without additional resources has resulted in many welfare officers moving into conciliation without receiving any specific training in its concepts and skills, even though their training for civil work itself may be scanty. James and Wilson's (1983) survey of probation officers' training found that social work qualifying courses and in-service training did not prepare officers adequately for marital and family work. Only 58 per cent of the officers questioned said they received some training on their qualifying courses on the impact of marital breakdown on adults and children, and only 50 per cent had received equivalent in-service training. Just on a quarter said they had had no training for civil work at any stage and 82 per cent expressed a need for more training for work which they found particularly difficult and demanding.

Conciliation and court-referred work with families (welfare inquiries, matrimonial supervision orders, guardian *ad litem* work, adoption) call for interdisciplinary knowledge and skills which go well beyond the limited training resources available to most agencies. In many areas, conciliation schemes have developed from joint initiatives taken by judges, registrars, probation officers, solicitors and social workers, and it is important to build on these partnerships between parent disciplines. Conciliation is developing as a new hybrid discipline and it would be unfortunate if one parent discipline took sole custody, care and control of the conciliation 'infant' and denied the essential involvement of other disciplines. Just as children need two parents who are able to work together, families need social workers and lawyers who understand each other's perspectives and concerns. There is considerable scope for cross-fertilisation between different disciplines in developing new approaches, and instead of wasting time and energy on territorial battles, we need to identify more precisely the knowledge base and skills needed by practitioners. Short training courses building on previous training and experience could be organised in five related sections:

1. knowledge base;
2. principles and tasks;
3. methods and skills;
4. consultation, supervision and support systems;
5. liaison and joint work with other agencies.

1. Knowledge base

Conciliators, court welfare officers and guardians *ad litem* need at least basic knowledge of the following subjects:

family systems and the family life-cycle; child development and children's reactions to conflict and loss; the process and dimensions of divorce and changing relationships in separated families and stepfamilies; matrimonial and family law and court procedures; sources of advice and assistance on welfare rights and housing; cultural and ethnic traditions which bear on parents' decisions about their children; and knowledge of the help available locally from voluntary and statutory agencies. Much of this knowledge may have been acquired through previous training and practical experience but trainees will probably need to extend and update what they already know. They may also need help to integrate these disparate areas of knowledge in a theoretical framework which can encompass them in a flexible way. An eclectic approach based on systems theory can combine concepts drawn from different sources such as crisis theory, structural and strategic family therapy, conflict theory and attachment theory. Knowledge of these theoretical perspectives increases awareness of different approaches and may prevent over-reliance on one limited approach.

This knowledge base is extensive but trainees should be recruited from people who already have relevant training and experience. A check-list can then be used to identify particular gaps in their knowledge so that they can take the modules they need and have credits for others. For example, a social worker with previous training in family therapy but no experience of court work could take a module on law and court procedures whereas someone with more legal knowledge might concentrate on family systems theory and family processes in separation and divorce. Short courses can be run on a regional basis and can be self-financing if offered to adjoining regions.

2. *Principles and tasks*

However experienced social workers may be in related fields of work, the move into conciliation calls for some exploration of personal values and basic principles. A conscious shift is required from one role to another, since conciliation and mediation involve a 'discontinuation of habits and assumptions fostered by the mediator's original profession. This step requires a change in the internal map which guides us to our philosophical destination' (Folberg and Taylor, 1984, p. 237). The territory of marital conflict and family break-up may be the same, but a conciliator moves over it in a different way from a reporting officer or family therapist. Ethical as well as practical issues need to be explored fully, such as whose values determine what tasks should be addressed and in what way.

Hypothetical situations can be devised to help workers consider their own values and responses to complex and controversial issues. The DHSS Report on Social Work Decisions in Child Care (1985b) found that social work judgements were often based on unexamined values and assumptions variously drawn from the worker's social class and cultural background, life experience, professional training and agency policy. This report emphasises that social workers need to examine and discuss the values they bring to their work, to reduce the influence of unconscious bias or preconceptions.

3. *Methods and skills*

Practical skills are probably developed more effectively through experiential learning than by didactic teaching. Some agencies rely on 'sitting-by-Nellie' methods in which trainees are apprenticed to experienced workers. This can have disadvantages, however, as such a lot depends on 'Nellie'. She may have quirks which the trainee dares not question or be so skilled that the trainee feels less confident than before. Videotapes, live supervision and role-play help develop skills and although each of these methods has some drawbacks, they can encourage peer-group learning and team support. Role-playing each stage of an interview can focus on micro-skills, such as the phrasing of a question or when and how to control an emotional tirade. Concentrating on one stage at a time (introductions, explaining the help being offered, clarifying issues and problems, exploring options, negotiations, etc) helps trainees develop skills on a step-by-step basis and may reduce anxiety about managing the whole process at once. After each role-play, training groups can discuss the skills they observed being used, what seemed to facilitate the process and what alternative strategies or interventions might have been equally or more useful.

Dowling and colleagues (1982) evaluated student training at the Family Insitute in Cardiff, asking students to rate the relevance of different components of the training they received on a five-point scale ranging from 'not at all relevant' to 'extremely relevant'. Their replies showed that they valued experiential learning – practice, supervision, observed interviews and videotapes – far more highly than theoretical learning. This survey indicated that task-focused, skills-oriented programmes helped students develop basic skills which they were able to apply in a variety of work settings.

Basic skills in working with families during separation and divorce include convening and engaging couples and families; clarifying, assessing and ranking issues; planning the pace of work; giving information and exploring options; reframing; communicating with children; balancing unequal power while discussions take place; containing conflict; supporting individuals while relating to the family as a whole; translating and summarising; referring to or co-working with other professionals and agencies. Intensive short courses or workshops can focus on specific skills, combining group discussion with video and role-play.

4. Agency support systems, including consultation and supervision

The quality of the help we offer families is strongly influenced by the functioning of our agency and the level of support available to its staff. Consultation and supervision are key elements of this support, though the differences between them are not always understood very well. Kingston and Smith (1983) defined consultation in family therapy as a 'situation in which the second person has some authority of expertise but no power to implement it without the invitation and permission of the therapist; the relationship is basically one between professional peers whose concerns are mutual, namely the satisfactory progress and outcome of therapy through increasing skill' (p. 220). A consultant offers additional insight and support without being responsible to the agency for the worker's management of a case. The same applies to co-work with colleagues, although this is sometimes misleadingly referred to as 'live supervision'.

A supervisor differs from a consultant in being formally accountable to the agency for the worker's professional practice, while also providing support and sharing responsibility for difficult decisions. The Beckford Inquiry Report (1985) emphasised that supervision is essential even for experienced workers. Although the Report was primarily concerned with child abuse, its definition of the supervisor's main functions is also relevant to other social work contexts including conciliation and welfare inquiries. These functions are:

(a) ensuring that the worker has the necessary knowledge and skills,
(b) monitoring the worker's activities,
(c) being aware of the attitudes of the worker towards a case with a view to correcting the handling of it if necessary,
(d) supporting the worker both practically and emotionally.

Vernon and Fruin (1985) found considerable confusion in social services departments as to whether the role of a team leader and/or supervisor is primarily to support the team or to carry out a management function in ensuring high standards of work, with the threat of discipline if necessary. Nearly one in five social workers in Vernon and Fruin's study was dissatisfied with the supervision they received, and the DHSS Report on Social Work Decisions in Child Care (1985b) reached the depressing conclusion that supervisors often failed to provide either real support or appropriate controls. The Report observed that social work managers generally did not appreciate the high levels of stress which fieldworkers experience in working face to face with their clients. Although this report focused on social work practice in childcare cases, its findings apply with equal force to social work in separation and divorce, where the levels of stress are also extremely high. Workers at the sharp end of family conflict need support from colleagues as well as from seniors;

those who work in isolated outposts may not get support from anyone.

The importance of good support cannot be overemphasised, since work with warring parents and their families is very draining and our fund of patience, goodwill and understanding cannot be limitless. We know we should not take sides, and yet the appalling injustice of some situations evokes a partisan response. We know we should not tell people what to do, but may find ourselves giving directive advice. And we book appointment after appointment and then wonder why we are feeling so stressed. It is heartrending to see a 3-year-old screaming at the sight of her father, whom she accepted and loved only a few months before. We have to try to retain our sensitivity and imagination, even though this makes us vulnerable to other people's anguish. If we block off this vulnerability and offer standardised responses, our capacity to reach and help people will be severely limited. Sometimes it is the very strength of our reaction which is the problem, rather than lack of concern: it can be very hard sometimes not to feel angry or alienated when someone seems to be acting cruelly or irresponsibly. The effort to keep our feelings in check can sap our physical and mental energy. If we drive ourselves too hard and fail to get adequate support, the price may be illness, nervous exhaustion and deteriorating relationships with colleagues.

Consultants and supervisors may help us cope with these reactions but case discussions often focus on the problems of a particular family, without exploring their personal impact on us. As Zetzel (1985) says, when we work with families, we bring an invisible cast of 'extras' – our own partners, parents, in-laws, siblings, children, friends and colleagues – who have shaped our experiences and expectations of relationships. Our reactions to marital and parental conflict may be partly unconscious. Even if we recognise their source, it may be difficult to explore deeply personal feelings with a supervisor who is assessing one's performance and promotion prospects. There is also the practical difficulty that the supervisor or consultant may not be available just when we need them most. Anxiety and anger about not coping with one's work well enough may be deflected elsewhere, by blaming other people, maintaining a tight-lipped silence or firing off sharp retorts – in other words, the very reactions our clients often show in the crisis of marital breakdown.

We need to recognise these reactions in ourselves and in our colleagues, so that the emotional load can be shared and levels of stress kept within manageable limits. It is very helpful after an exhausting session to let off steam to a sympathetic colleague who can reassure, joke or just commiserate. Team meetings can increase the cohesion and resilience of the team, provided there is good communication and enough trust to deal with interpersonal issues that may seem threatening to individuals. Some teams make a point of relaxing together at regular intervals by going out to a pub or restaurant, though family commitments tend to restrict the amount of time that can be spent with colleagues outside working hours. But there is enough evidence of serious breakdown in working relationships to suggest that preventive work is needed to avoid the risk of bitter and adversarial divorces taking place in our own agencies. A strong peer group is the best insurance against this happening, with access to a consultant who is a resource for the group as a whole. Conciliation techniques can be used by the consultant if the group shows signs of splitting, to reduce the risks of blaming and scapegoating if the group becomes divided. However, some workers are isolated geographically and do not have any colleagues within reach, and seniors who carry heavy responsibilities in their agency may also feel isolated. Team leaders and directors often lack someone they can talk to freely at their own level of seniority, without worrying about possible repercussions on staff above and below them. Senior staff who feel unfairly criticised may become exhausted, resentful and depressed and this may deplete their strength and self-confidence to a dangerous extent.

Liaison and joint work with other agencies

One way of buttressing individual workers at different levels of seniority is for agencies to link up with each other for peer group support and in-service training. Team leaders and coordinators of voluntary agencies in the same city or district may find they have much in common although the nature of their work differs. Regular informal meetings may be very supportive and provide an opportunity for brainstorming and management consultancy. Agencies may also join forces to run day conferences or short training courses. These events provide opportunities to share experience and problems, reviving flagging energies and stimulating interest in new ideas. In some areas, probation officers specialising in court-referred conciliation meet with conciliators from a voluntary agency to discuss general issues and concerns, without running into problems of agency confidentiality.

An inter-agency support group which meets on a monthly basis can also provide a pool of co-workers that can supplement scarce resources in each other's agency. It is not always feasible to co-work on a regular basis but it may be possible to enlist a co-worker to help with a particular difficult case. In one such case, a child and a family guidance social worker who was working with a separated mother and her children was perceived by the father as being on the mother's side. He refused to come to a family meeting convened by this worker but when a worker in another agency whom he had contacted made the same proposal, it was possible to arrange a meeting with the whole family and both workers. Co-working may also be helpful where a family is from a different ethnic background from the worker. If a worker from another agency acts as a consultant or co-worker in relation to these ethnic issues, it is essential to clarify the relative status and responsibilities of each worker. They may have different concerns and the practice of their agencies – on confidentiality, for example – may differ. It is important to establish beforehand whether one worker is acting only as a consultant to the other or whether they are sharing equal responsibility for the case.

Partnerships between statutory and voluntary agencies need not threaten the autonomy of either service. The philosophy of conciliation encourages joint working and co-operation between agencies offers a model of negotiation and joint decision-making which parallels the model we may be using with separated families. If we work in this way, some additional resources are needed for training and consultancy but workers may find they are able to work more effectively, with less strain than they would otherwise experience.

Educating children in conflict management

Social workers spend a lot of effort and time providing first aid to the casualties of divorce. Comparatively little preventive work is done to reduce the incidence of these casualties but there are some exciting developments, such as the use of forum theatre in schools as a method of teaching 'creative conflict resolution'. This method, derived from work with adults by the Brazilian Augusto Boal, is being used in workshops for schoolchildren by a psychotherapist called Michael Soth, under the aegis of the Institute for Social Inventions (*Guardian*, 25 May 1986). Once a week, Michael Soth worked with a class of 7- and 8-year-olds, getting them to re-enact a quarrel or fight and then role-playing it a second time. During the second role-play, any child in the class could shout 'stop' and take over one of the roles, showing how it could be managed differently. Positive ways of behaving were rehearsed and discussed and the children became so involved in their drama sessions that they decided to give a demonstration to the school assembly. By the end of term, their class teacher reported that although there were still a couple of isolated children, relationships in the class were greatly improved and disagreements were sorted out more easily. If conflict management were made a basic part of the school curriculum, like reading and writing, it could be taught by experiential methods at all ages and applied to many different kinds of family and social conflict. Utopia will always be a long way off, but many children can learn how to disagree and still listen to each other, without having to declare all-out war. In helping them acquire and apply this much-needed learning, maybe we adults could learn more of it ourselves.

Appendix A

Some Books about Divorce for Children

Althea (1980) *I have two homes* (Dinosaur). Pre-school age.

Blume, Judy (1972) *It's not the end of the world* (Piccolo). Story of a 12-year-old girl whose parents split up.

Children's Society. *Bruce's Story*.

Hogan, Paula (1980) *Mum, Will Dad Ever Come Back?* (Blackwell, Oxford, Raintree). A story about a girl's feelings when her parents split up – she runs away from home but there is a reassuring ending.

Leeson, Robert (1980) *It's My Life* (Fontana Lions). Good for teenagers. In this family it is the mother who leaves home.

McAfee, Analena and Anthony Browne. *The Visitors Who Came to Stay* (Hamish Hamilton). A good story, beautifully illustrated and written from a child's point of view about her feelings when her father, with whom she lives after her parents' divorce, acquires a new partner who also has a child from a previous marriage. Suitable for children aged 8–14.

Mitchell, Ann (1986) *When Parents Split Up: Divorce explained to Young People* (Chambers paperback). Written for children aged 10–15, this book offers helpful explanations which parents could also use in talking to younger children about divorce, custody decisions, etc.

Nystrom, Carolyn (1986) *Mike's Lonely Summer* (Lion Care Series). Child's guide through divorce, has a religious basis.

Snell, Nigel *Sam's New Dad* (Hamish Hamilton). For younger children.

Appendix B

Some Useful Addresses

Children's Legal Centre,
20 Compton Terrace,
London N1 2UN

Families Need Fathers
84 Ullswater Road,
Southgate,
London N14 7BT

Family Courts Campaign,
c/o National Children's Bureau
8 Wakley Street,
London EC1V 7QE

Family Rights Group,
6–9 Manor Gardens,
Holloway Road,
London N7

Forum for Initiatives in Reparation
and Mediation (FIRM)
Secretary, Rose Ruddick,
4 Grosvenor House,
Grosvenor Road,
Coventry CV1 3FZ

Gingerbread,
35 Wellington Street,
London WC2.

Mothers Apart From Their
Children (MATCH),
64 Delaware Mansions,
Delaware Road,
London W9.

National Council for One Parent
Families,
255 Kentish Town Road,
London NW5 2LX

National Family Conciliation
Council,
34 Milton Road,
Swindon, Wilts SN1 5JA

Scottish Council for Single Parents,
13 Gayfield Square,
Edinburgh

Solicitors' Family Law Association,
Secretary, P. H. Grose-Hodge,
154 Fleet Street,
London EC4A 2HX

Stepfamily (National Step-Family
Association),
Room 3,
Ross Street Community Centre,
Ross Street,
Cambridge CB1 3BS

References

Ahrons, C. A. (1980) 'Redefining the Divorced Family: A Conceptual Framework', *Social Work*, vol. 25, pp. 437–41.

Ambrose, P., Harper J., Pemberton R. (1983) *Surviving Divorce – Men Beyond Marriage*, Brighton, Wheatsheaf Books.

Anderson, M. (1983) 'What is new about the modern family?', in *The Family*, OPCS Occasional Paper 31, London, OPCS.

Ballard, R. (1982) 'South Asian Families', in R. N. Rapoport, M. P. Fogarty, and R. Rapoport (eds) *Families in Britain*, London, Routledge & Kegan Paul.

Beckford Inquiry Report (1985) *A Child in Trust*, London, Borough of Brent.

Bell, K. (1973) *Disequilibrium in Welfare*, Newcastle, University of Newcastle Octave.

Benians, R. (1986) 'Psychiatric Work with Reconstituted Families', *Family Law* vol. 16, pp. 60–4.

Bentovim A. and Gilmour, L. (1981) 'A family therapy interactional approach to decision making in child care, access and custody cases', *Journal of Family Therapy*, vol. 3, pp. 65–77.

Bentovim, A., Gorell Barnes, G., Cooklin, A. (eds) (1982) *Family Therapy: Complementary Frameworks of Theory and Practice*, London, Academic Press.

Bernard, J. (1973) *The Future of Marriage*, Harmondsworth, Penguin.

Binney, V., Harkell, G., and Nixon, J. (1985) 'Refuges and Housing for Battered Women', in J. Pahl (ed.) *Private Violence and Public Policy*, London: Routledge & Kegan Paul.

Bohannan, P. (1970) *Divorce and After*, New York, Doubleday.

Booth Committee (Committee on Matrimonial Causes Procedure) (1985) *Report*, London, HMSO.

Borkowski, M., Murch, M., Walker, V. (1983) *Marital Violence – The Community Response*, London, Tavistock.

Bottomley, A. and Olley, S. (1983) 'Conciliation in the USA', *Legal Action Group Bulletin*, January 1983, pp. 9–11.

Bowlby, J. (1969, 1973, 1980) *Attachment and Loss*, Vols 1–3, London, Hogarth Press.

159

Brannen, J. and Collard, J. (1982) *Marriages in Trouble*, London, Tavistock.

British Association of Social Workers, (1985) *Family Courts – A Discussion Document*, Birmingham, BASW.

Burgoyne, J. (1985) 'Gender, Work and Marriage: Patterns of Continuity and Change', in C. Guy (ed.) *Relating to Marriage*, Rugby, National Marriage Guidance Council.

Burgoyne, J. and Clark, D. (1982) 'Reconstituted families', in R. N. Rapoport, M. F. Fogarty, R. Rapoport (eds) *Families in Britain*, London, Routledge & Kegan Paul.

Burgoyne, J. and Clark, D. (1984) *Making a Go of It – A Study of Stepfamilies in Sheffield*, London, Routledge & Kegan Paul.

Cantwell, B. (1986) 'After Booth – Whither Conciliation and the Welfare Report?' *Family Law*, vol. 16, pp. 278–80.

Caplan, G. (1985) 'Recent Developments in Crisis Intervention and in the Promotion of Support Systems', unpublished paper.

Carpenter, J. and Treacher, A. (1983) 'On the neglected but related arts of convening and engaging families and their wider systems', *Journal of Family Therapy*, vol. 5 (4), pp. 337–59.

Carter, E. A. and McGoldrick, M. (eds) (1980) *The Family Life Cycle*, New York, Gardner Press.

Central Statistical Office (1986) *Social Trends 16*, London, HMSO.

Chester, R. (1971) 'Health and Marriage Breakdown – experience of a sample of divorced women', *British Journal of Preventive and Social Medicine*, vol. 25 (4), pp. 231–5.

Clulow, C. (1982) *To Have and to Hold: Marriage, the first baby and preparing couples for parenthood*, Aberdeen, Aberdeen University Press.

Clulow, C. and Vincent, C. (1987) *Divorce Court Welfare and the Search for Settlement*, London, Tavistock.

Cseh-Szombathy, L., Koch-Nielson, I., Trost J., Weda, I. (eds) (1985) *The Aftermath of Divorce – Coping with Family Change*, Budapest, Akademiai Kiado.

Davis, G. (1982a) 'Conciliation – A Dilemma for the Divorce Court Welfare Service', *Probation Journal*, vol. 29, no. 4.

Davis, G. and Bader, K. (1982b) 'In-Court Mediation on Custody and Access Issues at Bristol County Court – The Observation Study', Department of Social Administration, University of Bristol.

Davis, G. (1983) 'Conciliation and the Professions', *Family Law*, 13 (1), pp. 6–13.

Davis, G. (1985) 'The Theft of Conciliation', *Probation Journal*, vol. 32 (1), pp. 7–10.

Davis, G., MacLeod, A., and Murch, M. (1982) 'Divorce and the Resolution of Conflict', *Law Society's Gazette*, 13 January 1982, pp. 40–1.

Davis, G., MacLeod, A. and Murch, M. (1983a) 'Undefended Divorce: Should Section 41 of the Matrimonial Causes Act 1973 be Repealed?', *Modern Law Review*, 46, p. 121.

Davis, G., MacLeod, A. and Murch, M. (1983b) 'Divorce: Who Supports the Family?', *Family Law*, vol. 13, pp. 217–24.

Denning Committee, (1947) *Final Report of the Committee on Procedure in Matrimonial Causes*, London, HMSO, Cmnd. 7024.

Department of Health and Social Security, (1983) *Code of Practice: Access to Children in Care*, London, HMSO.

Department of Health and Social Security (1985a) *Review of Child Care Law*, London, HMSO.

Department of Health and Social Security (1985b) *Social Work Decisions in Child Care: Recent Research Findings and their Implications*, London, HMSO.

Department of Health and Social Security (1986) *Children in Care in England and Wales March 1984*, London, HMSO.

Deutsch, M. (1973) *The Resolution of Conflict*, New Haven, Yale University Press.

Dicks, H. (1967) *Marital Tensions*, reprinted in paperback 1983, London, Routledge & Kegan Paul.

Dimmock, B. and Dungworth, D. (1985) 'Beyond the Family: using network meetings with statutory child care cases', *Journal of Family Therapy*, 7, pp. 45–68.

Dobash, R. E., Dobash, R. P. and Cavanagh, K. (1985) in J. Pahl (ed.) *Private Violence and Public Policy*, London, Routledge & Kegan Paul.

Dodds, M. (1983) 'Children and Divorce', *Journal of Social Welfare Law*, July 1983, pp. 228–37.

Dowling, E., Cade, B., Breunlin, D. C., Frude, N. and Seligman, P. (1982) 'A retrospective survey of students' views on a family therapy training programme', *Journal of Family Therapy*, 4, pp. 61–72.

Eekelaar, J. (1982) 'Children in Divorce: Some Further Data', *Oxford Journal of Legal Studies*, 63.

Eekelaar, J. (1984) *Family Law and Social Policy*, 2nd edn, London, Weidenfeld & Nicolson.

Eekelaar, J. (1985) 'Parents and Children: rights, responsibilities and needs', *Adoption and Fostering*, vol. 9. pp. 7–10.

Eekelaar, J. and Clive, E. with Clarke K. and Raikes S. (1977) *Custody After Divorce*, Oxford, SSRC Centre for Socio-Legal Studies.

Ewbank, J. (1985) Transcript of judgment in the case of Wendy Heart (A Minor), High Court of Justice, Manchester, 19 December 1985.

Family Courts Campaign, (1986) 'A Court Fit For Families', London, unpublished paper.

Family Policy Studies Centre (1987) *One Parent Families*, Fact Sheet 3, London, FPCS.

Ferri, E. (1984) *Stepchildren*, Windsor, NFER-Nelson.

Finer Report (1974) *Report of the Committee on One-Parent Families*, London, HMSO, Cmnd 5629.

Folberg, J. (1984) (ed.) *Joint Custody and Shared Parenting*, Washington, Bureau of National Affairs.

Folberg, J. and Taylor, A. (1984) *Mediation, – A Comprehensive Guide to Resolving Conflicts Without Litigation*, San Francisco, Jossey-Bass.

Francis, P. and Shaw, R. (1981) 'Divorce and the Law and Order Lobby', *Family Law*, vol. 11, pp. 69–72.

Freeman, M. (1984) 'Questioning the De-Legalisation Movement in Family Law: Do We Really Want a Family Court?' in J. Eekelaar and S. Katz (eds) *The Resolution of Family Conflict – Comparative Legal Perspectives*, Toronto, Butterworth.

Frontenac Family Referral Service (1984) *Couples in Crisis II*, Kingston, Ontario, Frontenac Family Court.

Gibson, C. (1982) 'Maintenance in the Magistrates' Courts in the 1980s', *Family Law*, vol. 12, p. 138.

Gibson, P. and Parsloe, P. (1984) 'What stops parental access to children in care?', *Adoption and Fostering*, vol. 8 (1), pp. 18–24.

Goldman, J. and Coane, J. (1977) 'Family Therapy after the Divorce: Developing a Strategy', *Family Process*, pp. 357–62.

Gorell Barnes, G. (1984) *Working With Families*, London BASW/Macmillan.

Gorer, G. (1971) *Sex and Marriage in England Today*, London, Nelson.

Griew, E. and Bissett-Johnson, A. (1975) 'Supervision Orders in Matrimonial and Guardianship Cases', *Social Work Today*, vol. 6 (11), pp. 322–5.

Guise, J. (1983) 'Conciliation: Current Practice and Future Implications for the Probation Service', *Probation Journal*, vol. 30 (2), pp. 58–60.

Haley, J. (1976) *Problem Solving Therapy*, New York, Harper & Row.

Hancock, E. (1980) 'The dimensions of meaning and belonging in the process of divorce', *American Journal of Orthopsychiatry*, vol. 50 (1), pp. 18–27.

Hart, N. (1976) *When Marriage Ends: A Study in Status Passage*, London, Tavistock.

Haskey, J. (1984) 'Social Class and Socio-economic Differentials in Divorce in England and Wales', *Population Studies*, vol. 38, pp. 419–38.

Haynes, J. M. (1981) *Divorce Mediation*, New York, Springer Publishing Company.

Haynes, J. M. (1982) 'A Conceptual Model of the Process of Family Mediation: Implications for Training', *American Journal of Family Therapy*, vol. 10 (4), pp. 5–16.

Hetherington, E. M., Cox, M. and Cox, R. (1982) 'Effects of Divorce on Parents and Children', in M. E. Lamb (ed.) *Non-Traditional Families: Parenting and Child Development*, London, Academic Press.

Hodder, E. (1985) *The Step-Parents Handbook*, London, Sphere Books.

Hoggett, B. (1981) *Parents and Children*, London, Sweet & Maxwell.

Holman, R. (1973) *Trading in Children*, London, Routledge & Kegan Paul.

Holmes, T. H. and Rahe, R. H. (1967) 'The social readjustment rating scale', *Journal of Psychosomatic Research*, vol. 11.

Home Office, (1984) *Statement of National Objectives and Priorities for the Probation Service in England and Wales*, London, Home Office.

Home Office (1986) *Summary Probation Statistics, England and Wales*,

1985, London, Home Office Statistical Bulletin, 7 August 1986.

Houghton Committee (1970) *The Adoption of Children*, London, HMSO.

House of Commons Social Services Committee (1984) *Second Report on Children in Care*, Vol. 1, London, HMSO.

Howard, J. and Shepherd, G. (1982) 'Conciliation – New Beginnings?', *Probation Journal*, vol. 29 (3), pp. 87–92.

Howard, J. and Shepherd, G. (1987) *Conciliation, Children and Divorce*, London, Batsford/BAAF.

Hunt, P. (1985) *Clients' Responses to Marriage Counselling*, Rugby, National Marriage Guidance Council.

Interdepartmental Review of Family and Domestic Jurisdiction (1986), London, Lord Chancellor's Department.

Jackson, C. (1986) 'Mediation is not Conciliation', *Family Law*, vol. 16, pp. 357–8.

James, A. and Wilson, K. (1983) 'Divorce Court Welfare Work – Present and Future?' *Probation Journal*, vol. 30 (2), pp. 50–5.

James, A. and Wilson, K. (1984) 'The Trouble with Access: A Study of Divorcing Families', *British Journal of Social Work*, vol. 14, pp. 487–506.

James, A. and Wilson, K. (1986) *Couples, Conflict, and Change*, London, Tavistock.

Jewett, C. (1984) *Helping Children Cope with Separation and Loss*, London, Batsford/BAAF.

Jordan, P. (1985) *The Effects of Marital Separation on Men*, Brisbane, Family Court of Australia.

Justice, (1975) *Parental Rights and Duties and Custody Suits*, London, Stevens & Sons.

Kell, H. (1986) 'The guardian ad litem in access proceedings', *Adoption and Fostering*, vol. 10 (2), p. 16–18.

Kelly, J. B. and Wallerstein, J. (1977) 'Brief Interventions with Children in Divorcing Families', *American Journal of Orthopsychiatry*, vol. 47 (1), pp. 23–39.

Kessler, S. and Bostwick, S. (1977) 'Beyond divorce: coping skills for children', *Journal of Clinical Child Psychology*, vol. 6, pp. 38–41.

Kiernan, K. E. (1983) 'The structure of families today: continuity or change?' in OPCS Occasional Paper 31, *The Family*, London, OPCS.

King, M. (1981) 'Justice and Welfare in Divorce', *Legal Action Group Bulletin*, March issue.

Kingston, P. and Smith, D. (1983) 'Preparation for live consultation and supervision when working without a one-way screen', *Journal of Family Therapy*, vol. 5 (3), pp. 219–33.

Kitson, G. C., Lopata, H. Z., Holmes, W. M., Meyering, S. M. (1980) 'Divorcees and Widows: similarities and differences', *American Journal of Orthopsychiatry*, vol. 50 (2), pp. 291–310.

Kitson, G. C. and Sussman, M. B. (1977) 'The Impact of Divorce on Adults', *Conciliation Courts Review*, vol. 15, pp. 20–4.

Kitson, G. C. and Sussman, M. B. (1982) 'Marital Complaints, Demographic Characteristics and Symptoms of Mental Distress in Divorce',

Journal of Marriage and the Family, February 1982, pp. 87–101.

Kitson, G. C., Graham, A. V., Schmidt, D. D. (1983) 'Troubled Marriages and Divorce', *Journal of Family Practice*, vol. 17 (2), pp. 249–58.

Kitson, G. C. and Langlie, J. K. (1984) 'Couples who file for divorce but change their minds', *American Journal of Orthopsychiatry*, vol. 54, (3), pp. 469–89.

Krementz, J. (1985) *How It Feels When Parents Divorce*, London, Gollancz.

Kressel, K. (1985) *The Process of Divorce – How Professionals and Couples Negotiate Settlements*, New York, Basic Books.

Kressel, K. and Deutsch, M. (1977) 'Divorce Therapy: an in-depth survey of therapists' views', *Family Process*, vol. 16 (4), pp. 413–43.

Kressel, K. and Deutsch, M., Jaffe, N., Tuchman, B., Watson, C. (1980) 'A Typology of Divorcing Couples', *Family Process*, vol. 19 (2), pp. 101–16.

Langsley, D. G., Kaplan, D., Pittmann, F. S., Machotka, P., Flomenhaft, K. and Deyoung, C. (1968) *The Treatment of Families in Crisis*, New York, Grune & Stratton.

Law Commission (1986) *Review of Child Law: Custody*, London, HMSO.

Law Commission (1987) *Care, Supervision and Interim Orders in Custody Proceedings*, Working Paper No. 100, London, HMSO.

Law Society's Standing Committee on Family Law (1986) *A Suggested Model for the Family Court*, London, October 1986.

Leete, R. and Anthony, S. (1979) *Divorce and Remarriage*, Population Trends 16, London, HMSO.

Leicestershire Divorce Court Welfare Service (1979) 'The Divorce Experience Course – a guide for staff members', unpublished paper.

Levin, J. (1984) 'Maintenance problems and priorities' in M. Freeman (ed.) *The State, The Law and the Family*, London, Tavistock.

Lindemann, E. (1965) 'The Symptomatology and Management of Acute Grief' in H. J. Parad (ed.) *Crisis Intervention*, New York, Family Service Association.

Little, M. (1982) *Family Breakup*, San Francisco, Jossey-Bass.

Loftus, Y. (1986) 'Black families and parental access', *Adoption and Fostering*, vol. 10 (4), pp. 26–7.

Lord Chancellor's Legal Aid Advisory Committee (1983) *32nd Annual Report 1981–82*, London, HMSO.

Lund, M. (1984) 'Research on Divorce and Children', *Family Law*, vol. 14, pp. 198–201.

McCoy, K. F. and Nelson, M. A. (1983) *Social Service Departments and the Matrimonial Causes (NI) Order*, Belfast, Social Work Advisory Group.

Maclean, M. and Eekelaar, J. (1983) *Children and Divorce: Economic Factors*, Oxford, SSRC Centre for Socio-Legal Studies.

MacGillavry, D. and Bijkerk, H. (1986) 'An Experimental Approach to Divorce Assistance: Recent Developments in the Netherlands', *Mediation Quarterly*, no. 11, pp. 109–18.

Maddox, B. (1980) *Step-parenting: How to live with other people's children*, London, Allen & Unwin.

Maidment, S., 'A Study in Child Custody', *Family Law*, vol. 6 (1976), pp. 195, 236.

Maidment, S. (1981) *Child Custody – What Chance for Fathers?*, London, National Council for One-Parent Families.

Maidment, S. (1984) *Child Custody and Divorce: The Law in Social Context*, London, Croom Helm.

Maluccio, A. (1979) *Learning from Clients: Interpersonal Helping as viewed by clients and social workers*, New York, Free Press.

Marshall, A., Grant, A. and Nasser, J. (1979) 'Children's Wishes in Custody and Access Disputes', *Australian Social Work*, vol. 31 (4), pp. 15–18.

Martin, F. and Murray, K. (1984) 'Principles, Practice and Policy in the Juvenile Justice System', *The Scottish Child*, January, pp. 6–10.

Masson, J. (1984) 'Old families into new: a status for step-parents', in M. Freeman (ed.) *The State, the Law and the Family*, London, Tavistock.

Mattinson, J. and Sinclair, I. (1979) *Mate and Stalemate*, Oxford, Basil Blackwell.

Mayer, J. and Timms, N. (1970) *The Client Speaks*, London, Routledge & Kegan Paul.

Maynard, M. (1985) 'The response of social workers to domestic violence' in J. Pahl (ed.) *Private Violence and Public Policy*, London, Routledge & Kegan Paul.

Millham, S., Bullock, R., Hosie, K. and Gower, M. H. (1985) 'Children Lost in Care', see DHSS Report (1985b) *Social Work Decisions in Child Care*, London, HMSO.

Minuchin, S. (1974) *Families and Family Therapy*, Cambridge, Mass.; Harvard University Press.

Mitchell, A. (1981) *Someone to Turn to – Experiences of Help before Divorce*, Aberdeen, Aberdeen University Press.

Mitchell, A. (1985) *Children in the Middle – Living Through Divorce*, London, Tavistock.

Mnookin, R. (1984) 'Divorce Bargaining: The Limits on Private Ordering', in J. Eekelaar and S. Katz (eds) *The Resolution of Family Conflict – Comparative Legal Perspectives*, Toronto, Butterworth.

Mnookin, R. and Kornhauser, L. (1979) 'Bargaining in the Shadow of the Law – The Case of Divorce', *Yale Law Journal*, vol. 88, p. 950.

Montalvo, V. and Haley, J. (1973) 'In defence of child therapy', *Family Process*, vol. 12, pp. 227–44.

Moore, J. (1982) 'Like a rabbit caught in headlights', *Community Care*, vol. 436, pp. 18–20.

Morgan, H. G. (1979) *Death Wishes?*, Chichester, John Wiley & Sons.

Morley, A. (1985) 'Splitting Up – Background and Aims', in C. Guy (ed.) *Relating to Marriage*, Rugby, National Marriage Guidance Council.

Moskoff, W. (1983) 'Divorce in the USSR', *Journal of Marriage and the Family*, May 1983, pp. 419–25.

Murch, M. (1980) *Justice and Welfare in Divorce*, London, Sweet & Maxwell.

National Association of Probation Officers (1984) Discussion paper on

conciliation, February, 1984.
National Association of Probation Officers (1985) Family courts policy document, November, 1985.
National Family Conciliation Council (1986) Code of Practice.
Nuffield Centre for Health Services Studies (1984) *Unemployment, Health and Social Policy*, Leeds, Nuffield Centre.
Oberg, B. and Oberg, G. (1982) *I'm Leaving*, London, Norman Hobhouse.
O'Brien, A. and Loudon, P. (1985) 'Redressing the Balance – involving children in family therapy', *Journal of Family Therapy*, vol. 7, pp. 81–98.
Office of Population Censuses and Surveys (OPCS) (1984a) *Marriages 1983*, London, HMSO.
OPCS (1984b) *General Household Survey*, London, HMSO.
OPCS (1986a) *Adoptions in England and Wales 1984*, London OPCS.
OPCS (1986b) *Divorces in England and Wales 1985*, London, OPCS.
O'Hagan, K. (1984) 'Family crisis intervention in social services', *Journal of Family Therapy*, vol. 6, pp. 149–81.
Oldfield, S. (1983) *The Counselling Relationship*, London, Routledge & Kegan Paul.
Pahl, J. (1985) 'Violent Husbands and Abused Wives' in J. Pahl (ed.) *Private Violence and Public Society*, London, Routledge & Kegan Paul.
Palazzoli, M. S. (1984) 'Behind the scenes of the organisation', *Journal of Family Therapy*, vol. 6, pp. 229–307.
Palazzoli, M. S. (1985) 'The Emergence of a Comprehensive Systems Approach', *Journal of Family Therapy*, vol. 7, no. 2, pp. 135–46.
Palazzoli, M. S., Boscolo, L., Cecchin, G. and Prata, G. (1978) *Paradox and Counterparadox*, London and New York, Jason Aronson.
Palazzoli, M. S., Boscolo, L., Cecchin, G. and Prata, G. (1980) 'Hypothesising, circularity, neutrality', *Family Process*, vol. 19, pp. 3–12.
Papp, P. (1977) 'The family who had all the answers', in P. Papp (ed.) *Family Therapy: Full Length Case Studies*, New York, Gardner Press.
Parad, H. J. and Caplan, G. (1965) 'A Framework for Studying Families in Crisis', in H. J. Parad (ed.) *Crisis Intervention*, New York, Family Service Association of America.
Parkes, C. M. (1972) *Bereavement: Studies of Grief in Adult Life*, London, Tavistock.
Parkinson, L. (1981) *Joint Custody*, One Parent Times No. 7, London, National Council for One Parent Families.
Parkinson, L. (1983) 'Conciliation – A New Approach to Family Conflict Resolution', *British Journal of Social Work*, vol. 13, pp. 19–37.
Parkinson, L. (1985) 'Divorce counselling' and 'Conciliation in separation and divorce' in W. Dryden (ed.) *Marital Therapy in Britain*, vol. 2, London, Harper & Row.
Parkinson, L. (1986a) 'International Conference on Conciliation and Divorce', *Family Law*, vol. 16, pp. 287–9.
Parkinson, L. (1986b) *Conciliation in Separation and Divorce – Finding Common Ground*, London, Croom Helm.

Patrician, M. (1984) 'Child Custody Terms: Potential Contributors to Custody Dissatisfaction and Conflict', *Mediation Quarterly*, no. 3, pp. 41–57.

Pearce, B. (1985) 'Civil Work in the 1980s – a Surrey View', *Family Law*, vol. 15, pp. 302–4.

Pearce, N. (1986) *Wardship: The Law and Practice*, London, Fourmat Publishing.

Pearson, J. and Thoennes, N. (1984) 'Custody Mediation in Denver: Short and Longer Term Effects' in J. Eekelaar and S. Katz (eds) *The Resolution of Family Conflict – Comparative Legal Perspectives*, Toronto, Butterworth.

Pincus, L. (1976) *Death and the Family*, London, Faber.

Priest, J. A. and Whybrow, J. C. (1986) *Custody Law in Practice in the Divorce and Domestic Courts*, London, HMSO.

Priestley, J. M. (1984) 'Mediation Conferences – The New Zealand Family Court's Alternative to Litigation' in J. Eekelaar and S. Katz (eds) *The Resolution of Family Conflict – Comparative Legal Perspectives*, Toronto, Butterworth.

Principal Registry of the Family Division (1986) Practice Direction, *Children: Enquiry and Report by a Welfare Officer*, London, 28 July, 1986.

Probation Service (1986) *Probation Statistics 1985*, London, Home Office.

Pugsley, J. and Wilkinson, M. (1984) 'The Court Welfare Officer's Role: Taking it Seriously?', *Probation Journal*, vol. 31 (3), pp. 89–92.

Rapoport, L. (1965) 'The State of Crisis – some theoretical considerations' in H. J. Parad (ed.) *Crisis Intervention*, New York, Family Service Association.

Read, M. (1985) 'Splitting Up – The Course', in C. Guy (ed.) *Relating to Marriage*, Rugby, National Marriage Guidance Council.

Reid, W. and Epstein, L. (1972) *Task-Centred Casework*, New York, University Press.

Ricci, I. (1986), Paper given at the Annual Conference of the Association of Family and Conciliation Courts, Boston, USA, May 1986.

Richards, M. P. M. and Dyson, M. P. M. (1982) *Separation, Divorce and the Development of Children: A Review*, University of Cambridge, Child Care and Development Group.

Rimmer, L. (1982) 'Changing Patterns of Marriage and Remarriage' in S. Saunders (ed.) *Change in Marriage*, Rugby, National Marriage Guidance Council.

Roberts, S. (1983) 'Mediation in Family Disputes', *Modern Law Review*, vol. 46, no. 5, pp. 537–557.

Robinson, M. E. (1980) 'Step-families: a reconstituted family system', *Journal of Family Therapy*, vol. 2, pp. 45–69.

Rosen, R. (1977) 'Children of Divorce: what they feel about access and other aspects of the divorce experience', *Journal of Clinical Child Psychology*, Summer 1977, pp. 24–7.

Ross, J. (1985) 'The Place of Children in the Conciliation Process', *The Scottish Child*, issue no. 7, pp. 10–13.

Rowe, J. and Lambert, L. (1973) *Children Who Wait*, London, ABAA, now BAAF.

Rutter, M. (1971) 'Parent-Child Separation – Psychological Effects on the Children', *Journal of Child Psychology and Psychiatry*, vol. 12, no. 4, pp. 233–60.

Rutter, M. (1985) 'Resilience in the Face of Adversity', *British Journal of Psychiatry*, vol. 147, pp. 598–611.

Sager, C., Steer Brown, H., Crohn, H., Engel, T., Rodstein, E. and Walker, L. (1983) *Treating the Remarried Family*, New York, Brunner Mazel.

Saposnek, D. T. (1983) *Mediating Child Custody Disputes*, San Francisco, Jossey-Bass.

Seale, S. (1984) *Children in Divorce: A Study of Information Available to the Scottish Courts on Children Involved in Divorce*, Edinburgh, Scottish Office Central Research Unit.

Shepherd, G. and Howard, J. (1985a) 'Custody, Access and Home Visits', *Family Law*, vol. 15, pp. 136–7.

Shepherd, G. and Howard, J. (1985b) 'Theft or Conciliation? The Thieves Reply', *Probation Journal*, vol. 32 (2), pp. 59–60.

Smart, C. (1984) 'Marriage, divorce and women's economic dependency' in M. Freeman (ed.) *The State, the Law and the Family*, London, Tavistock.

Smith, D. and Kingston, P. (1980) 'Live supervision without a one-way screen', *Journal of Family Therapy*, vol. 2, pp. 379–87.

Social Trends 16 (1986), London, HMSO.

Solicitors' Family Law Association (1984) Code of Practice, *Family Law*, vol. 14, pp. 156–7.

Southwell, M. (1985) 'Children, Divorce and the Disposal of the Matrimonial Home' *Family Law*, vol. 15, pp. 184–6.

Steinberg, J. L. (1980) 'Towards an interdisciplinary commitment', *Journal of Marital and Family Therapy*, pp. 259–67.

Steinman, S. (1981) 'The Experience of Children in a Joint Custody Arrangement', *American Journal of Orthopsychiatry*, vol. 51, pp. 403–14.

Stone, L. (1977) *The Family, Sex and Marriage in England 1500–1800*, London, Weidenfeld & Nicolson.

Stone, N. (1986) 'Is there a role for the probation service?', *Adoption and Fostering*, vol. 10 (2), pp. 37–40.

Taylor, P. M. (1984) 'Conciliation – Divide and Rule?', *Family Law*, vol. 14, pp. 300–2.

Terkelson, K. (1980) 'Towards a Theory of the Family Life Cycle' in E. Carter and M. McGoldrick (eds) *The Family Life Cycle*, New York, Gardner Press.

Thorpe, R. (1980) 'The Experiences of Children and Parents Living Apart', in J. Triseliotis (ed.) *New Developments in Foster Care and Adoption*, London, Routledge & Kegan Paul.

Tyndall, N. (1985) 'The Work and Impact of the National Marriage Guidance Council' in W. Dryden (ed.) *Marital Therapy in Britain*, vol. 1, London, Harper & Row.

Vernon, J. and Fruin, D. (1985) *In Care – A Study of Social Work Decision-Making*, London, National Children's Bureau.

Visher, E. B. and Visher, J. S. (1979) *Stepfamilies: a guide to working with stepfamilies and stepchildren*, New York, Brunner Mazel.

Visher, E. B. and Visher, J. S. (1985) 'Stepfamilies are different', *Journal of Family Therapy*, vol. 7, pp. 9–18.

Walczak, Y. with Burns, S., (1984) *Divorce: the Child's Point of View*, London, Harper & Row.

Walker, J. and Wray. S. (1986) Papers given at the Transatlantic Conference on Conciliation, London School of Economics, 27–28 May, 1986.

Wallerstein, J. (1982) 'Children of Divorce: Preliminary Report of a Ten-Year Follow-Up', paper presented in Dublin, July 1982.

Wallerstein, J. and Kelly, J. B. (1977) 'Divorce Counseling – A Community Service for Families in the Midst of Divorce', *American Journal of Orthopsychiatry*, vol. 47 (1), pp. 4–22.

Wallerstein, J. and Kelly, J. B. (1980) *Surviving the Breakup – How Children and Parents Cope with Divorce*, London, Grant McIntyre.

Walrond-Skinner, S. (1976) *Family Therapy: The Treatment of Natural Systems*, London, Routledge & Kegan Paul.

Watzlawick, P., Beavin, J., Jackson, D. (1967) *Pragmatics of Human Communication*, New York, W. W. Norton.

Watzlawick, P., Weakland, J., Fisch, R. (1974) *Change: Principles of Problem Formation and Problem Resolution*, New York, W. W. Norton.

Weakland, J., Fisch, R., Watzlawick, P., and Bodin, A. (1974) 'Brief therapy focused problem resolution', *Family Process*, vol. 13, pp. 141–68.

Weeda, I. (1985) 'The significance of the social network after separation' in L. Cseh-Szombathy, I. Koch-Nielsen, J. Trost, and I. Weeda, *The Aftermath of Divorce – Coping with Family Change*, Budapest, Akademiai Kiado.

Weiss, R. S. (1975) *Marital Separation*, New York, Basic Books.

West Midlands Probation Service (undated) 'Asian Marriages and the Welfare Services', unpublished paper.

Whitaker, C. A. (1977) 'Process Techniques of Family Therapy', *Interaction*, vol. 1, pp. 4–19.

Whitaker, C. A. and Miller, M. H. (1969) 'A re-evaluation of psychiatric help when divorce impends', *American Journal of Psychiatry*, vol. 126, pp. 57–64.

Wilkinson, M. (1981) *Children and Divorce*, Oxford, Basil Blackwell.

Winnicott, C. (1977) 'Communicating with Children', *Social Work Today*, vol. 8 (26), pp. 7–11.

Woman magazine (1982) *A Survey of Divorced Couples*, 27 February, 1982.

Zetzel, G. W. K. (1985) 'In and Out of the Family Crucible: Reflections on Parent–Child Mediation', *Mediation Quarterly*, vol. 7, pp. 47–67.

Index

access
  access centres 69
  access orders in Northern
    Ireland 72
  access orders in Scotland 72
  children's refusal 53–5, 60,
    63, 65–7
  common problems 18–19, 51–
    5, 62, 65–70, 117, 120, 128
  length of visits 51, 54
  loss of contact 18–19, 56–7
  reasons for continuing access
    57–8, 119, 130–1
  to children in care xvi, 130–1
adversarial system in divorce 8,
  11, 16–17, 74, 89, 136
Asian families xv, 63, 97
assessment of family problems
  29–31, 38–46, 83–6, 90,
  141
Association of Chief Officers of
  Probation 92, 147
attachment 15, 28–9, 39–40,
  120–2, 130–1
Australia, Family Court
  counsellors 63, 139

battered women 29–31, 43–6
  see also domestic violence
Beckford Inquiry Report 152
bereavement see loss
black families 97, 122, 125
Booth Report 75, 90, 123–4

Canada, family courts 141
child abuse xvi, 32, 80, 86, 98,
  111, 152
children
  communicating with children
    48–52, 62–5, 88
  groupwork with children 69–
    70
  in care 130–1, 137, 145
  interpreting children's reactions
    52–5
  roles in family conflict 58–62,
    66–70, 120–2
  the wishes of the child 62–7
  welfare in divorce 71–3, 91
circular questioning 107
Citizens' Advice Bureau 32
cohabitees xv, 1, 110–12, 133
conciliation xvi, 17, 23–4, 41,
  93–118, 149–50
  and welfare inquiries 89, 95,
    139–41, 146–7
  imbalances in conciliation 46,
    100–1, 108–9, 143–4
  in childcare cases 146
  including children 63–5
  legally privileged 90
  on finance and property 98
  organisational settings 95–8
  time-out during sessions 105
  use of authority 96, 99
  women's position 46, 100–1
  see also co-working, training

Conciliation Project Unit 99
confidentiality 31–2, 61–2, 90–2, 98
conflict
    disagreement between professionals 10, 77, 80, 88, 91, 154
    children's reactions 49–50, 119–21, 134–5
    conflict management 11–12, 23–4, 28–9, 35–6, 40–6, 93–5, 112–18, 156
    in divorce 14–7, 23–4
    intractable conflict 42–3, 86–7, 122
    patterns of post-divorce conflict 38–43
conjoint work 12–13, 23–4, 27–31, 39–46, 80
consultation in social work 104–8, 151–4
convening couples and families 12–13, 27–32, 61–2, 68, 108–10, 144–5
counselling *see* divorce counselling
court welfare officers *see* welfare officers
co-working xvi, 30, 43, 97, 101–8, 127
    interdisciplinary co-working xvii, 14, 97, 155
crisis intervention 26–30, 35–6, 42, 45–6
    theory 26
custodianship 76, 138
custody orders 73–8, 134, 136–8, 140
    see also joint custody

divorce
    adversarial system 74, 89, 136
    and loss 6–7, 22, 35, 57–8
    and poverty 7, 17–19, 25
    and unemployment 25
    checking arrangements for children 71
    counselling 9, 65, 99

decree nisi and decree absolute 6
different dimensions of divorce 14–22
disputes 14–19, 74–5
divorce experience courses 23, 41, 70
    impact on children 49–52, 120–1
    parenting after divorce 3, 16, 55–7, 74–5, 88, 130–5
    rates 1, 25–6
    reform 16–17, 78, 136
domestic courts 18, 75–6, 79, 95, 123–5, 136–7
domestic supervision orders 92, 122–30
domestic violence 10, 19, 29, 31, 43–6

enmeshed couples 15, 42–3, 121
ethnic minorities xiv–v, 66, 97, 155
    different cultural traditions 86, 97, 149

family
    changing patterns 3–5
    courts 17, 94, 136–42, 146–7
    diversity of families in Britain xiv, 132
    dynamics 55, 58–61, 66
    life-cycle 25, 133, 149
    meetings 64–5, 81, 83, 89, 91, 127–9, 143
    restructuring after divorce xiii, xvii, 4–5, 16, 67–9, 78, 130–2
    systems 6, 13, 46, 59, 106–8, 149
    therapy 5, 59, 64, 69, 88, 98–9, 103, 109
    see also Asian families, black families, Jewish families
fathering 4–5, 18–19, 56–7, 67–8, 74–5, 133
feminist views of conciliation 101
Finer Report 94, 138

gender issues for social workers 102
genograms 113
general practitioners 10–11, 20, 31, 58
grandparents 20, 58, 76, 137
groupwork
  divorce experience courses 23, 41, 70
  network meetings 144–5
  with children 69–70, 156
guardians *ad litem* xvi, 147, 148

home visits 83, 89, 101
humour 115

injunctions 44, 137
intake issues 108–10, 140–1

Jewish families 97
joint custody 18, 76–8, 126
judicial separation 17

Law Commission 72–3, 76–8, 123, 125
legal aid 16–17, 116
loss in divorce 6, 19, 22–3, 35, 57–8

magistrates *see* domestic courts
maintenance payments 17–19, 105, 137
marital violence *see* domestic violence
marriage guidance–8–9, 11, 96
matrimonial supervision orders *see* supervision orders
mediation 89, 91, 103, 107, 127, 140
  between families and the court 83
  see also conciliation
Milan method 106–8

National Family Conciliation Council 98
network meetings 38, 46, 144–5

New Zealand, family courts 140–1
non-accidental injury *see* child abuse
Northern Ireland, divorces 72

one-parent
  families 5, 7, 17–20
  households 5, 7

paradoxical interventions 106–8
parenting after divorce 3–5, 9, 16–19, 55–7, 74–5, 88, 130–5
play materials 67–8
police 45
positive connotation *see* re-framing
pre-empting conflict 114–15
privilege in conciliation 90
Probation Service 9, 70, 78–92, 95, 122–3, 126
  see also welfare officers
psychoanalytic theory 4, 12

reconciliation 9, 22, 27, 79, 94
re-framing 105, 106, 117
remarriage 1–2, 21–2
role-play 30, 70, 150–1, 156

Scotland
  children's panels 143
  divorces 72, 77–8
sculpting 68
Section 41 appointments 71–2
single parents *see* one-parent families
social workers
  gender issues 102
  need for support xii, xvi, 30, 151–5
  role of consultant 104–8, 151–4
  supervision 151–4
  training 30, 43, 144, 147–51
solicitors 9, 11, 17, 43, 76, 88
  in mediation 97–8

Solicitors' Family Law Association 17, 98
stepfamilies xv, 5, 21, 29, 58, 132–5
step-parents 5, 58, 76, 115, 128–30, 132–5, 145–6
stress
associated with separation xii–iii, 6–7, 19–20
effects on individuals 6–7, 21–3
experienced by social workers xii, 24, 152–3
in families 3, 7, 21, 25–7, 119–22, 132–5
suicide 7, 25, 41
supervision orders in family proceedings 92, 122–30, 137
systems theory 6, 13, 37, 46, 149

task-centred approach 36, 42, 87
time-scale of work 24, 84–5, 99, 118, 123, 127
training for conciliation and court

welfare work 30, 98, 144, 147–51

unemployment 25

video, use in training 150–1
violence 29–31, 51, 56
risks to social workers 101
see also domestic violence

wardship 71, 123, 137–8
welfare inquiries and conciliation 81–1, 89–92, 95–8, 107–8, 139–41, 146–7
welfare officers 62–4, 72, 78–92, 99, 121–3, 147–8
welfare rights 18
women
as mothers 3–5, 44
as single parents 5, 7, 18–20
in conciliation 101
in society 3, 44, 101
see also battered women